LawExpress
MEDICAL LAW

MEDICAL LAW

4th edition

Jonathan Herring
Professor of Law, Exeter College, University of Oxford

Harlow, England • London • New York • Boston • San Francisco • Toronto • Sydney • Auckland • Singapore • Hong Kong
Tokyo • Seoul • Taipei • New Delhi • Cape Town • São Paulo • Mexico City • Madrid • Amsterdam • Munich • Paris • Milan

Pearson Education Limited
Edinburgh Gate
Harlow
Essex CM20 2JE
England
and Associated Companies throughout the world.

Visit us on the World Wide Web at:
www.pearson.com/uk

First published 2008 (print)
Second edition 2010 (print)
Third edition published 2013 (print)
Fourth edition published 2015 (print and electronic)

ISBN: 978-1-292-01288-9 (print)
     978-1-292-01342-8 (PDF)
     978-1-292-01306-0 (eText)
     978-1-292-01810-2 (ePub)

British Library Cataloguing-in-Publication Data
A catalogue record for this book is available from the British Library

Library of Congress Cataloging-in-Publication Data
A catalog record for this book is available from the Library of Congress

10 9 8 7 6 5 4 3 2 1
17 16 15 14

Print edition typeset in 10/12pt Helvetica Neue LT Pro by 35
Print edition printed and bound in Malaysia (CTP-PPSB)

NOTE THAT ANY PAGE CROSS REFERENCES REFER TO THE PRINT EDITION

Contents

Acknowledgements   vii

Introduction   viii

Guided tour   x

Guided tour of the companion website   xii

Table of cases and statutes   xiv

Chapter 1:   Basic principles of medical law and ethics   1

Chapter 2:   Rationing   13

Chapter 3:   Consent to treatment   25

Chapter 4:   Confidentiality   41

Chapter 5:   Medical negligence   52

Chapter 6:   Contraception, abortion and pregnancy   65

Chapter 7:   Reproduction   79

Chapter 8:   Organ donation and ownership of body parts   94

Chapter 9:   Death and dying   106

Chapter 10:   Mental health law   121

Chapter 11:   Medical research   132

And finally, before the exam . . .   141

Glossary of terms   146

Index   149

Supporting resources

Visit the *Law Express* series companion website at **www.pearsoned.co.uk/lawexpress** to find valuable student learning material including:

- A **study plan** test to help you assess how well you know the subject before you begin your revision
- Interactive **quizzes** to test your knowledge of the main points from each chapter
- Sample **examination questions** and guidelines for answering them
- Interactive **flashcards** to help you revise key terms, cases and statutes
- Printable versions of the **topic maps** and **checklists** from the book
- **'You be the marker'** allows you to see exam questions and answers from the perspective of the examiner and includes notes on how an answer might be marked
- **Podcasts** provide point-by-point instruction on how to answer a typical exam question

Also: The companion website provides the following features:

- Search tool to help locate specific items of content
- E-mail results and profile tools to send results of quizzes to instructors
- Online help and support to assist with website usage and troubleshooting

For more information please contact your local Pearson Education sales representative or visit **www.pearsoned.co.uk/lawexpress**

Acknowledgements

I am grateful to all those at Pearson Education who work on this series. In particular, Donna Goddard, Christine Statham and Rebekah Taylor, who have provided invaluable guidance on the format and flavour of the books. I am also very grateful to my wife Kirsten and daughters Laurel, Jo and Darcy for all their love, support and distraction during the writing of this book.

Jonathan Herring

Publisher's acknowledgements

Our thanks go to all reviewers who contributed to the development of this text, including students who participated in research and focus groups which helped to shape the series format.

Introduction

Medical law is a fascinating subject. It raises all kinds of interesting debates and different clashes of principle. It is certainly a topic on which people tend to have very strong views. In fact, beware, you can lose friends if you get too heated discussing these ethical principles! But listening to others respectfully can teach you about a variety of different ways of understanding the world, our bodies and the power of medicine.

Because it can be such a controversial area, students can get carried away when writing exams. There are three dangers, in particular. First, in the exam hall, do not write a rant instead of an essay. Remember, you do not know the views the person marking the exam will have and so it is dangerous to be too rude about those you disagree with. However strong your opinions, you should consider the variety of approaches to a topic in a sensitive way. This is not to say that your essay should simply summarise the beliefs of others and not make clear your own thoughts. Many essay questions will ask you to set out your perspective on a controversial issue. But in doing so you can explain the views of others and why you do not find them convincing. Second, it is easy to end up writing an essay which fails to mention any law at all. As you will be taking a law exam, this is not a very good idea! So make sure wherever possible that you are referring to relevant statutory provision or case law. Even if your essay question is more theoretical, show how theoretical debates become relevant in particular cases. Third, there is a danger in polarising debates into two extremes whereas, in fact, there may be several compromise positions available. Abortion is an area where the debate often breaks down into two camps: pro-life or pro-choice. There is, however, middle ground between these two views. That said, you may well conclude that such compromise positions are 'messy' and indicate indecisiveness and a failure to deal with the issues. Still, beware of presenting ethical debates as simply a choice between two extreme views.

There are a number of themes which run across the different topics covered in this book and in most medical law courses. For example, the extent to which patients have the right to decide whether or not to receive treatment; the moral and legal status of the embryo; the extent to which patients have rights and responsibilities. These issues raise their heads at a number of places in a medical law course. In an essay question in an exam, it can be interesting to demonstrate how an issue which is raised in one topic reflects debates that appear in other subjects. In other words, don't see medical law as being made up of a number of discrete boxes which have nothing to do with each other. Rather it involves the balancing of different principles and values in a variety of different contexts.

The primary aim of this book is to help you to revise for your exams. To be honest, if so far you have done no work, attended no lectures, and read no other material, you will get little help here. If, however, you have been doing some work but are feeling overwhelmed by the amount of material available and are unsure how to put it together in order to revise for the exam, this is the book for you. A first-class answer is likely to include references to more cases than are found in these pages and will discuss more theoretical issues than are discussed here. What this book can do is to set you off on the right path for your revision. It will help you see the wood for the trees and emphasise the points that you must know. Hopefully, most of the material you will have come across before, but it will help put it in some kind of order and help you see how it can be used to answer questions in the exam. If you have read and understood this book, you will have at your fingertips the key cases and principles to do well in the exam.

📖 **REVISION NOTE**

Make sure you are aware of up-to-date changes in legislation, as several areas of medical law are in flux at the moment.

Be careful of overlapping areas of law – both within the medical law area and between medical and other types of law – and make sure you shape your answer around the focus of the question. Also, when revising with cases that involve medical and non-medical areas of law, be careful to focus on the relevant aspects of the judgment.

Before you begin, you can use the study plan available on the companion website to assess how well you know the material in this book and identify the areas where you may want to focus your revision.

Guided tour

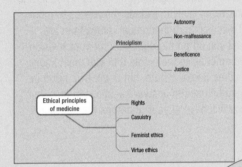

Topic maps – Visual guides highlight key subject areas and facilitate easy navigation through the chapter. Download them from the companion website to pin on your wall or add to your own revision notes.

Revision checklists – How well do you know each topic? Use these to identify essential points you should know for your exams. But don't panic if you don't know them all – the chapters will help you revise each point to ensure you are fully prepared. Print the checklists off the companion website and track your revision progress!

Revision checklist

Essential points you should k

- [ ] Some of the key approaches to r
- [ ] The key legal principles governin
- [ ] How ethical principles and mer

Sample questions with answer guidelines – Practice makes perfect! Read the question at the start of each chapter and consider how you would answer it. Guidance on structuring strong answers is provided at the end of the chapter. Try out additional sample questions online.

Assessment advice – Not sure how best to tackle a problem or essay question? Wondering what you may be asked? Use the assessment advice to identify the ways in which a subject may be examined and how to apply your knowledge effectively.

Key definitions – Make sure you understand essential legal terms. Use the flashcards online to test your recall!

■ Sample question

Could you answer this question? Below is a typical essay question that could arise on this topic. Guidelines on answering the question are included at the end of this chapter. Another sample question and guidance on tackling it can be found on the companion website.

ESSAY QUESTION

Is it useful to develop key ethical principles governing medical issues? Is it possible to develop an effective way of reconciling clashes between these principles?

ASSESSMENT ADVICE

An essay question is likely to ask you to assess some of the leading ethical principles. You will need to describe them and give examples of how they are reflected in legal principles. You may also need to consider whether there are problems with the principles and the clashes that arise between them. For example, should autonomy be regarded as an overarching principle? There is also the debate over whether it is desirable to have general principles that are applied, or whether it is preferable to treat each case individually. An essay question might require you to consider how the law interacts with the different ethical principles. Should legal responses always match the ethical ones? Good answers will show how the disputes over these general principles are reflected in real cases, using examples from the case law.

KEY DEFINITION: Principle of beneficence

Medical professionals must provide the best medical treatment for their patients.

Key cases and key statutes – Identify and review the important elements of the essential cases and statutes you will need to know for your exams.

KEY STATUTE

Mental Capacity Act 2005
A person is not to be treate
unwise decision.

KEY CASE

Simms v. *Simms* [2003] 1 All ER 669
Concerning: when experimental surgery was lawful

Facts

Two teenagers were suffering from variant Creutzfeldt-Jakob Disease. Their doctors proposed a novel treatment which had not been tested on humans. The expert evidence suggested that the effectiveness of the surgery was unknown. Without the treatment,

Make your answer stand out – This feature illustrates sources of further thinking and debate where you can maximise your marks. Use them to really impress your examiners!

✓ Make your answer stand out

Many writers have supported the principle of autonomy. However, a good answer will emphasise that the principle of autonomy is not without its critics, at least as an absolute principle. Should a patient be permitted to refuse to consent to treatment even if this will mean that a huge burden will be placed on the patient's family to care for them? (See Herring, 2007.) Do patients not have responsibilities as well as rights? (See Brazier, 2006.) Further, is it right that patients should be able to refuse treatment if this

Exam tips – Feeling the pressure? These boxes indicate how you can improve your exam performance when it really counts.

⚛ EXAM TIP

Although the principle of beneficence sounds straightforward, it does raise some interesting issues. Should patients who want to be given treatment which is not in their best interests, but who are willing to pay for it, be denied the treatment? For example, should there be much greater restrictions on cosmetic surgery? What if a patient objects on religious grounds to a proposed treatment and wants a far less effective alternative?

Revision notes – Get guidance for effective revision. These boxes highlight related points and areas of overlap in the subject, or areas where your course might adopt a particular approach that you should check with your course tutor.

📖 REVISION NOTE

The principle of autonomy is particularly important when considering the legal requirement that a patient gives consent to treatment. (This is discussed in Chapter 3.) You will see there that the law strongly protects the right of a patient to refuse treatment.

Don't be tempted to . . . – This feature underlines areas where students most often trip up in exams. Use them to spot common pitfalls and avoid losing marks.

❗ Don't be tempted to . . .

You need to be careful when discussing an ethic of care. Initially, an ethic of care sounds very attractive. There are good arguments to be used in favour of taking account of the interests of carers when making medical decisions (see Herring (2007)). However, we also know that those who are meant to be caring for relatives do abuse them. There is a danger that relatives can manipulate the notion of an ethic of care to take advantage of older people. So if you want to promote an ethic of care you will

Read to impress – Focus on these carefully selected sources to extend your knowledge, deepen your understanding, and earn better marks in coursework as well as in exams.

READ TO IMPRESS

Beauchamp, T. and Childress, J. (2012) *Principles of Biomedical Ethics*. Oxford: Oxford University Press.

Brazier, M. (2006) 'Do No Harm – Do Patients Have Responsibilities Too?', 65 *Cambridge Law Journal* 397.

Foster, C. (2011) *Human Dignity in Bioethics and the Law*. Oxford: Hart.

Gillon, R. (2003) 'Ethics Needs Principles – Four Can Encompass the Rest – and Respect for

Glossary – Forgotten the meaning of a word? This quick reference covers key definitions and other useful terms.

Glossary of terms

The glossary is divided into two parts: key definitions and other useful terms. The key definitions can be found within the chapter in which they occur, as well as in the glossary below. These definitions are the essential terms that you must know and understand in order to prepare for an exam. The additional list of terms provides further definitions of useful terms and phrases

Guided tour of the companion website

Book resources are available to download. Print your own **topic maps** and **revision checklists**!

Use the **study plan** prior to your revision to help you assess how well you know the subject and determine which areas need most attention. Choose to take the full assessment or focus on targeted study units.

'**Test your knowledge**' of individual areas with quizzes tailored specifically to each chapter. **Sample problem and essay questions** are also available with guidance on writing a good answer.

Flashcards test and improve recall of important legal terms, key cases and statutes. Available in both electronic and printable formats.

'You be the marker' gives you the chance to evaluate sample exam answers for different question types and understand how and why an examiner awards marks.

Download the **podcast** and listen as your own personal Law Express tutor guides you through answering a typical but challenging question. A step-by-step explanation on how to approach the question is provided, including what essential elements your answer will need for a pass, how to structure a good response, and what to do to make your answer stand out so that you can earn extra marks.

All of this and more can be found when you visit **www.pearsoned.co.uk/lawexpress**

Table of cases and statutes

■ Cases

A Local Authority v. Mrs A and Mr A [2010] EWHC 1549 (Fam) 31, 32, 39

A London Local Authority v. JH [2011] EWHC 2420 (Fam) 36

A, B and C v. Ireland [2010] ECHR 2032 73

A-G v. Guardian Newspapers Ltd [1990] 1 AC 109 45

Airedale National Health Service Trust v. Bland [1993] AC 789 112, 118

AN NHS Trust v. SR [2012] EWHC 3842 (Fam) 38

Attorney-General's Reference (No. 3 of 1994) [1998] AC 245 75

B (Adult: Refusal of Medical Treatment), Re [2002] 2 FCR 1 107, 112

Bolam v. Friern Hospital Management Committee [1957] 2 All ER 118 33, 53, 54, 56, 57, 63

Bolitho v. City and Hackney Health Authority [1998] AC 232 58, 63

C (Adult: Refusal of Treatment), Re [1994] 1 WLR 290 26, 29

Campbell v. Mirror Group Newspapers [2004] UKHL 22 42, 45, 46, 50

Chatterton v. Gerson [1981] QB 432 31

Chester v. Afshar [2004] UKHL 41 33, 55, 60, 61, 63

DD v. Durham County Council [2013] EWCA Civ 96 124

Department of Health v. Information Commissioner [2011] EWHC 1430 (Admin) 47

DL v. A Local Authority [2012] EWCA Civ 253 34

Dorset CC v. EH [2009] EWHC 784 (Fam) 34

E (A Minor), Re [1993] 1 FLR 386 38

Ecclestone v. Medway NHS Trust [2013] EWHC 790 (QB) 57

Evans v. Amicus Healthcare [2004] 3 All ER 1025, CA 80, 85

Evans v. UK [2006] 1 FCR 585, ECtHR 80, 85, 86

F (In Utero), Re [1988] Fam 122 75

F v. West Berkshire Health Authority [1989] 2 All ER 545 56

Glass v. UK [2004] 1 FCR 553 116

Gillick v. West Norfolk and Wisbech Area Health Authority [1985] 2 WLR 413 26, 75, 137

Goodwill v. BPAS [1996] 2 All ER 161 56

Gregg v. Scott [2005] UKHL 2 53, 59, 60, 61

H (A Healthcare Worker) v. Associated Newspapers [2002] EWCA Civ 195 49

Haas v. Switzerland (Application 31322/07), January 2011 115

HL v. UK (2004) 40 EHRR 761; [2004] ECHR 45508/99 122, 128

Hotson v. East Berkshire Area Health Authority [1987] AC 750 59

J (A Minor), Re [1990] 3 All ER 930 116

Jepson v. Chief Constable of West Mercia [2003] EWHC 3318 72

Ingram v. Williams [2010] EWHC 758 (QB) 57

KB (Adult) (Mental Patient: Medical Treatment), Re (1994) 19 BMLR 144 127

L (A Child), Re [2010] EWHC 3146 (Fam) 88

M v. Blackpool Victoria Hospital NHS Trust [2003] EWHC 1744 (QB) 58

M v. F [2013] EWHC 1901 (Fam) 89

MB (An Adult: Medical Treatment), Re [1997] 2 FCR 541 76, 77

MD v. Nottinghamshire Health Care NHS Trust [2010] UKUT 59 (AAC) 129

MH v. Secretary of State for Health [2005] UKHL 60 122, 125, 130

Marriott v. West Midlands Health Authority [1999] Lloyd's Med Rep 23 58

Ministry of Justice v. Carter [2010] EWCA Civ 694 57

Moore v. Regents of the University of California (1990) 793 P 2d 479 (Cal) 103

NHS Trust v. T [2004] EWHC 1279 (Fam) 32

NHS Trust A v. M [2001] Fam 348 112

Paton v. BPAS [1979] QB 276 73–5

Pretty v. UK [2002] 2 FCR 97 114, 115

R v. Adomako [1995] 1 AC 171 107, 113

R v. Arthur (1981) 12 BMLR 1 110

R v. Bourne [1939] 1 KB 687 70

R v. Cambridge Health Authority ex p. B [1995] 1 WLR 898 14, 19, 23

R v. Collins and Ashworth Hospital Authority ex p. Brady [2000] Lloyd's Rep Med 355 34

R v. Department of Health ex p. Source Informatics [2001] QB 424 47

R v. Inglis [2010] EWCA Crim 2637 110

R v. Kelly [1998] 3 All ER 741 95, 102

R v. Marshall (2001) The Times, 29 September 113

R v. North West Lancashire Health Authority ex p. A [2000] 1 WLR 977 20, 21

R v. Tabassum [2000] 2 Cr App Rep 328 31

R v. Woollin [1999] 1 AC 82 110, 118

R (AC) v. Berkshire West Primary Care Trust [2011] EWCA Civ 247 22

R (Axon) v. Secretary of State for Health (Family Planning Association Intervening) [2006] EWHC 37 (Admin) 74, 75

R (B) v. Ashworth Hospital Authority [2005] 2 All ER 289 127

R (Burke) v. GMC [2005] 3 FCR 169 116

R (Condliff) v. North Staffordshire PCT [2011] EWHC 895 (Admin) 20

R (Eisai) v. National Institute for Health and Clinical Excellence [2008] EWCA Civ 438 21

R (Nicklinson) v. Ministry of Justice [2013] EWCA Civ 961 111

R (Pretty) v. DPP [2002] 1 AC 800 114, 115

R (Purdy) v. DPP [2009] UKHL 45 107, 114, 115, 119

R (Quintavalle) v. HFEA [2005] UKHL 28 80, 87

R (Rogers) v. Swindon NHS Primary Health Care Trust [2006] EWCA Civ 392 14, 21, 23

R (Sessay) v. South London and Maudsley NHS Trust [2011] EWHC 2617 (QB) 126

R (Smeaton) v. Secretary of State for Health [2002] 2 FCR 193 68, 69

R (Watts) v. Secretary of State for Health [2004] EWCA Civ 166 14, 22

Roe v. Minister of Health [1954] 2 QB 66 57

SB, Re [2013] EWHC 1417 (COP) 74

Sidaway v. Bethlem Royal Hospital Governors [1985] 1 All ER 643 32

Simms v. Simms [2003] 1 All ER 669 7, 133, 136

St George's Healthcare NHS Trust v. S [1998] 3 All ER 673 5, 34, 39, 66, 75–7

T (Adult: Refusal of Treatment), Re [1992] 3 WLR 782 32

T (A Child) (Surrogacy: Residence Order), Re [2011] EWHC 33 (Fam) 87

Tameside and Glossop Acute Services Trust v. CH [1996] 1 FCR 753 127

Thomas v. Curley [2013] EWCA Civ 117 58

Venables v. Mirror Group Newspapers [2001] 2 WLR 1038 45

Vo v. France (2005) 40 EHRR 12 75

W (A Minor) (Medical Treatment), Re [1992] 3 WLR 758 101

W v. Edgell [1990] 1 All ER 835 42, 48, 50

W v. M [2011] EWHC 2443 (Fam) 116

Wilsher v. Essex Area Health Authority [1987] QB 730 58

Wright v. Cambridge Medical Group [2011] EWCA Civ 669 58

Wyatt (A Child) (Medical Treatment: Continuation of Order), Re [2005] EWCA Civ 1181 116

X Primary Care Trust v. XB [2012] EWHC 1390 (Fam) 113

Y (Mental Incapacity: Bone Marrow Transplant), Re [1997] 2 FCR 172 37, 101

Yearworth v. North Bristol NHS Trust [2009] EWCA Civ 37 95, 103, 104

■ Statutes

Abortion Act 1967 67–73
  s. 1(1) 71
  s. 1(1)(a)–(d) 71, 72
  s. 1(3) 71
  s. 4 73
Access to Medical Reports Act 1998 50
Children Act 1989 87
Data Protection Act 1998 50, 136
Equality Act 2006 23
  s. 35 128
Equality Act 2010 22, 23
Health and Social Care Act 2001
  s. 60 47
Human Fertilisation and Embryology Act 1990 81–93, 103
  s. 3 84
  s. 3(2), (3) 84
  s. 3A 84
  s. 4 84
  s. 4(3) 84
  s. 11 87
  s. 13(5) 86
  s. 30 87, 88
  s. 41 84
  Sch 2 90
    para. 1(4) 84
  Sch 3 95
    para. 5 88
Human Fertilisation and Embryology Act 2008 86, 88, 90, 92
  s. 33 88, 93
  s. 35 89
  s. 35(1)(a), (b) 89
  s. 36 89
  s. 36(a) 89
  s. 36(b)–(d) 90
  s. 37 89, 90, 93
  s. 37(1)(a) 90
  s. 37(1)(b) 90, 91
  s. 37(1)(c)–(e) 90
  s. 37(2) 90
  s. 37(3) 90
  s. 38(2)–(4) 89, 90
  s. 41 88, 93
  s. 42 89, 91

  s. 42(1) 91
  s. 42(2) 91
  s. 43 91
  s. 43(a)–(c) 91
  s. 44 91
  s. 44(1)(a)–(d) 91, 92
  s. 44(1)(e) 92
  s. 44(2) 92
  s. 44(3) 92
  s. 45(2)–(4) 91
  Sch 6 89
Human Rights Act 1998 15, 46, 70, 74, 85, 106, 108, 112
Human Tissue Act 2004 94–102, 136, 147
  s. 1 98, 99, 102
  s. 1(1) 98
  s. 1(1)(a)–(g) 98
  s. 3 102
  s. 5 99
  s. 27 102
  s. 27(4) 108
  s. 32 102
  s. 33 100
  s. 33(1) 100, 101
  s. 33(1)(a), (b) 110
  s. 33(2) 110
  s. 33(2)(a), (b) 110
  s. 33(3) 110
  s. 33(3)(a), (b) 110
  s. 33(5) 110
  Sch 1 106–9
Infant Life (Preservation) Act 1929
  s. 1 76
Medicine Act 1968 67
Mental Capacity Act 2005 30, 31, 33, 34, 38, 40, 42, 43, 72, 83, 121, 135, 147
  s. 1(3) 33
  s. 2 34
  s. 2(1) 34
  s. 3(1) 34
  s. 4 41
  s. 4(6) 41
  s. 25 121
  s. 26(1) 39
  s. 30 147
  s. 31 147
  s. 31(1) 147

s. 31(5) 147
s. 32 147
s. 33 147
s. 33(2) 147
s. 34 147
Sch A1 41
Mental Health Act 1983 129, 131, 132, 135–7, 158
s. 1(2) 132, 158
s. 2 130, 133, 134
s. 2(2) 132
s. 2(2)(a), (b) 132
s. 3 130, 133, 134, 137
s. 3(2) 133
s. 3(2)(a) 133
s. 3 (2)(b), (c) 134
s. 4 130, 134
s. 64 135
s. 64D 135, 136
s. 64D(1) 135
s. 64D(2)–(5) 136
s. 118(2) 136, 137
s. 118(2)(a)–(i) 137
s. 145 137
Mental Health Act 2007 129, 131, 132, 135–8, 158
NHS Redress Act 2006 59, 66, 67
National Health Service Act 1977
s. 5(1)(b) 74
Offences Against the Person Act 1861
s. 58 75
s. 59 75
Road Traffic Act 1988
s. 172 52
Suicide Act 1961 123
s. 2(1) 122
Surrogacy Arrangements Act 1985
s. 1A 94

■ Statutory instruments

Abortion Regulations 1991, SI 1991/499 77
Human Tissue Act 2004 (Persons who Lack Capacity to
Consent and Transplants) Regulations 2006, SI
2006/1659 108
Public Health (Infectious Diseases) Regulations 1988,
SI 1988/1546 37

■ European and international legislation

Council Regulation 1408/71
Art. 22 25
EC Treaty
Art. 49 24, 25
European Convention on Human Rights 9, 79, 80, 123,
124, 138
Art. 2 9, 121, 123, 124
Art. 3 9, 121, 124, 138
Art. 5 133
Art. 8 9, 22, 49, 92, 123, 124
Art. 10 49
Art. 14 9, 26

Basic principles of medical law and ethics

1

Revision checklist

Essential points you should know:

- [ ] Some of the key approaches to medical ethics
- [ ] The key legal principles governing medical law
- [ ] How ethical principles and medical principles interrelate

■ Topic map

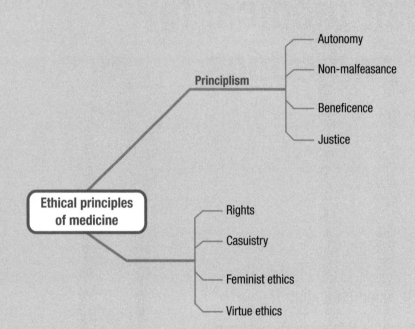

A printable version of this topic map is available from **www.pearsoned.co.uk/lawexpress**

■ Introduction

'Doctor knows best.'

This used to be a governing principle in medical law. In the past, doctors told patients what to do and patients obeyed. But nowadays there is much talk of the rights of patients and the responsibilities of doctors. What has not changed are the heated debates over the complex ethical issues that medicine raises. Some medical ethicists have produced a series of principles which they suggest can be applied to provide guidance in difficult cases. Other ethicists are less convinced that general rules can be developed and argue that it is better to fashion results that are right for individual cases. Although the law is influenced by ethical principles, it does not follow that the law and ethics match. It is unlikely that the law would require a medical professional to act in an unethical way. On the other hand, it cannot be assumed that just because something is legal it is also ethical.

ASSESSMENT ADVICE

An essay question is likely to ask you to assess some of the leading ethical principles. You will need to describe them and give examples of how they are reflected in legal principles. You may also need to consider whether there are problems with the principles and the clashes that arise between them. For example, should autonomy be regarded as an overarching principle? There is also the debate over whether it is desirable to have general principles that are applied, or whether it is preferable to treat each case individually. An essay question might require you to consider how the law interacts with the different ethical principles. Should legal responses always match the ethical ones? Good answers will show how the disputes over these general principles are reflected in real cases, using examples from the case law.

■ Sample question

Could you answer this question? Below is a typical essay question that could arise on this topic. Guidelines on answering the question are included at the end of this chapter. Another sample question and guidance on tackling it can be found on the companion website.

ESSAY QUESTION

Is it useful to develop key ethical principles governing medical issues? Is it possible to develop an effective way of reconciling clashes between these principles?

■ Consequentialism and deontology

Don't be frightened by these long words; the basic concepts behind them are not too difficult to grasp.

KEY DEFINITION: Consequentialism

This approach decides whether an act is ethically right or wrong by looking at its consequences. Quite simply, if it produces more good than bad, the act is ethically right.

KEY DEFINITION: Deontology

This approach says that it is right or wrong to infringe certain principles, regardless of the consequences. For example, some people believe it is never right to intentionally kill another person, however much good may be produced as a result.

A good example of where these two approaches might produce a different result is this. A doctor finds out that his patient is HIV positive. The patient refuses to tell his wife and intends to carry on having sexual relations with her. Should the doctor tell the wife about the husband's condition? A consequentialist may well answer 'yes'. The benefit of this will be that it will protect the wife from infection. Although the patient may be distressed, this will be less harm than that suffered by the wife. A deontologist may say there is an absolute principle that doctors must respect their patients' confidentiality. This principle should not be broken just because it will produce more good than harm.

✓ Make your answer stand out

A standard answer will explain the differences between consequentialism and deontology. A really good answer will argue that actually the distinction between the two is not as clear-cut as may, at first, be thought. For a consequentialist, are we to take into account that if the doctor tells the wife, patients as a group may start to trust their doctors less? This may have seriously bad consequences. Indeed, if a doctor breaches a moral principle (even if it produces a good result), this may lead to a loss in trust in the medical profession and so produce harmful results. This may mean that there is less difference between the approaches than may be thought. And might not the deontologist say that the governing principle is that, unless very serious harm will otherwise result, a confidence should be respected? This will lead to a position closer to that taken by the consequentialist.

◼ Four key ethical principles

In a highly influential book Tom Beauchamp and James Childress (2012) have suggested four principles which they say are a 'common morality'. In other words, they are principles which all societies should be able to accept. Their four principles are:

- respect for autonomy
- non-malfeasance
- beneficence
- justice.

Autonomy

Many ethicists believe that autonomy is the most important of all principles for medical ethics. It states that patients have the right to make decisions over what medical treatment they should receive. It is never permissible for a doctor to give a patient treatment without the patient's consent, unless the patient is incompetent, or maybe that is necessary to avoid serious harm to others. Even if the decision of the patient not to receive the treatment seems perverse or foolish, it must be respected (see Chapter 3 for further discussion).

Note, however, that respect of autonomy does not mean that patients have the right to demand treatment that they want. The law strongly respects the right of a patient to say 'no' (see Chapter 3), but not the right to demand treatment by saying 'yes' (see Chapter 2). The NHS could not afford to give patients every treatment they wanted.

An example of the principle of autonomy in practice is the following case.

KEY CASE

St George's Healthcare NHS Trust v. *S* [1998] 3 All ER 673

Concerning: whether it was lawful to perform a Caesarean section operation on a woman without her consent

Facts

S was 35 weeks pregnant when she was told she needed to have a Caesarean section operation. She was told that without one she and/or the fetus would die. She refused to consent. Her doctors assessed her competent to make the decision to refuse, but sought judicial approval to perform the operation. This was given by Hogg J, and a baby girl was born as a result. After the birth, the mother appealed against Hogg J's decision.

Legal principle

The Court of Appeal held that the mother's detention and the performance of the operation without her consent was unlawful. They confirmed that a competent woman had an absolute right to refuse treatment, this was not affected by the fact she was pregnant. If a competent pregnant woman refuses to consent to medical intervention, it cannot be imposed upon her. This is so even if without it she and the fetus will die.

📖 **REVISION NOTE**

The principle of autonomy is particularly important when considering the legal requirement that a patient gives consent to treatment. (This is discussed in Chapter 3.) You will see there that the law strongly protects the right of a patient to refuse treatment.

✓ Make your answer stand out

Many writers have supported the principle of autonomy. However, a good answer will emphasise that the principle of autonomy is not without its critics, at least as an absolute principle. Should a patient be permitted to refuse to consent to treatment even if this will mean that a huge burden will be placed on the patient's family to care for them? (See Herring, 2007.) Do patients not have responsibilities as well as rights? (See Brazier, 2006.) Further, is it right that patients should be able to refuse treatment if this will leave them in an undignified and distressing state? For example, should a patient be able to refuse to be washed while in hospital?

The principle of non-malfeasance

KEY DEFINITION: The principle of non-malfeasance

Medical professionals should not cause harm to their patients.

This principle is straightforward. Doctors must not harm their patients. At first it might be thought to be so obvious as to not need stating. However, it should be recalled that there can be a temptation in some cases to harm one patient in order to benefit another (e.g. by taking tissue for a transplant). This principle would not permit that. Some commentators argue that whether a procedure harms a patient depends on the patient's point of view. If a patient consents to the taking of an organ for transplantation, then it cannot be said to constitute harm. There is much to be said for that, but then it becomes hard to distinguish the non-malfeasance principle from the autonomy principle.

The following case demonstrates that it can be difficult sometimes to know whether a procedure will harm a patient.

KEY CASE

Simms v. *Simms* [2003] 1 All ER 669

Concerning: when experimental surgery was lawful

Facts

Two teenagers were suffering from variant Creutzfeldt-Jakob Disease. Their doctors proposed a novel treatment which had not been tested on humans. The expert evidence suggested that the effectiveness of the surgery was unknown. Without the treatment, the individuals would die. Their parents sought a declaration that it was lawful for the proposed treatment to be given.

Legal principle

Butler-Sloss P authorised the surgery. As the two teenagers were incompetent to make the decision, the question was simply whether doing the surgery would be in their best interests. She held that it was. Although medical opinion was divided on whether or not the treatment should be given, the experts agreed it would not be irresponsible to give the treatment. The chance of success might be slight, but, given they were facing death, it was a risk worth taking. She attached 'considerable weight' to the fact that the parents supported using the treatment.

The principle of beneficence

KEY DEFINITION: Principle of beneficence

Medical professionals must provide the best medical treatment for their patients.

In the current climate this is a problematic principle. The best treatment may be too expensive for the NHS to provide. (See the discussion of rationing of health care in Chapter 2.) Further, commentators add that this principle must be seen in conjunction with the principle of autonomy. Medical professionals cannot give a patient the best treatment against the wishes of the patient and then seek to rely on the principle of beneficence.

✎ EXAM TIP

Although the principle of beneficence sounds straightforward, it does raise some interesting issues. Should patients who want to be given treatment which is not in their best interests, but who are willing to pay for it, be denied the treatment? For example, should there be much greater restrictions on cosmetic surgery? What if a patient objects on religious grounds to a proposed treatment and wants a far less effective alternative?

The principle of justice

> **KEY DEFINITION: The principle of justice**
>
> Patients should be treated equally and fairly. One patient should not be improperly given preferential treatment over others.

While most people will agree that patients should be treated justly, there is much dispute over quite what this means. The dispute mostly comes to the fore in cases of rationing (which we shall look at in Chapter 2). If a young patient is given an expensive treatment, but an older patient suffering from the same medical condition is not, is this an infringement of the principle of justice?

✓ **Make your answer stand out**

Gillon (2003) provides a good summary of these principles. Note that he thinks that autonomy should be regarded as the most important principle. Some people are concerned that if, whenever there is a clash between autonomy and the other principles, autonomy wins out, then, in effect, there is only one principle (namely autonomy) and not four.

You should also be aware that some writers are sceptical of the benefits of developing principles that can be applied across the board (see, for example, Harris, 2003). A good exam answer will be able to explain the famous four principles but also be aware of the objections that have been raised against them.

■ Rights

The notion of **rights** in the medical arena has been of growing importance for ethicists and lawyers – for the latter, in particular, because of the Human Rights Act 1998.

> **KEY DEFINITION: Right**
>
> The concept of a right in law is much disputed and it is not possible to give a definition which would be accepted by everyone. When a person has a right to X, other people are bound by a duty to protect or promote the interests the person has in X. There need to be good reasons why the person should be prevented from X.

Some of the most important rights that can be found in the European Convention on Human Rights (ECHR) for medical lawyers include the following:

Right in the European Convention	Legal principle
Article 2: the right to life	A doctor may not intentionally kill a patient (see Chapter 9)
Article 3: the right to protection from torture, inhuman or degrading treatment	A doctor must not, where possible, leave a patient in a state which is inhuman or degrading
Article 8: the right to respect for private life	A patient has an absolute right to refuse treatment (see Chapter 3)
Article 8: the right to respect for family life	A doctor should consult with parents, where possible, before providing treatment to children (unless the child is sufficiently mature to make his or her own decision)
Article 14: the right not to be discriminated against	A doctor may not allocate healthcare resources based on age or sex

■ Casuistry

Casuistry emphasises that each case is different. It argues that rather than seeking to develop grand principles that apply across the board, each case should be considered in its own context. It is more effective to compare and contrast a case with similar ones, rather than seeking to apply a metaprinciple which applies across the board. The difficulty with such an approach is that it might be harder for doctors or other health professionals to determine what is ethically the correct approach if there are no general 'rules' to apply.

■ Dignity

For some commentators the notion of dignity is central to medical ethics (e.g. Foster, 2011). Dignity is a somewhat vague term, but relates to what it is about us that makes us human and requires us to respect each person's unique status. Therefore, even if a patient is happy to be left unwashed, they should not be because that would be to fail to respect their dignity and respect as a person. Dignity is also sometimes relied upon to explain why selling organs should not be permitted.

◼ Virtue ethics

Virtue ethicists emphasise that people should do the right thing and for the right reasons. A common way of approaching an issue is therefore to ask what character is manifested by a person acting in this way for this reason. So, for example, using a virtue ethics approach Hursthouse (1991) suggests that a woman who decides to have an abortion so that her holiday plans are not interfered with is not acting in a good way. Whereas a woman who had an abortion because she believed that the life of the child born would be intolerable would be acting in a virtuous way. Note that this would be so even if the woman's decision was based on a mistaken diagnosis by a doctor. Her character revealed by her act would be good (arguably), even if in fact the act did not produce a good (arguably).

◼ Feminist medical ethics

Feminist ethics emphasises that it is not possible to understand medical law and how it operates in practice without appreciating how it operates in a world of gender inequality. Feminist approaches have demonstrated how medicine and medical law have been used as ways of exercising power over women (e.g. through controlling them during pregnancy). Many feminist writers (e.g. Jo Bridgeman and Rosemarie Tong) have also promoted the use of an **ethic of care**.

KEY DEFINITION: Ethic of care

This is an ethical approach which emphasises that we all live in relationship with other people and are dependent upon other people. It is, therefore, not possible to look at a patient and ask what rights they have as a lone individual or what is best for the patient. Rather we need to ask what is best for this group of people who are in relationship together. It values interdependency and mutuality over individual freedom.

! Don't be tempted to . . .

You need to be careful when discussing an ethic of care. Initially, an ethic of care sounds very attractive. There are good arguments to be used in favour of taking account of the interests of carers when making medical decisions (see Herring (2007)). However, we also know that those who are meant to be caring for relatives do abuse them. There is a danger that relatives can manipulate the notion of an ethic of care to take advantage of older people. So if you want to promote an ethic of care you will need to explain how it can ensure that it can protect people from abuse.

■ Religious perspectives

Historically, and for many people still today, religious arguments have played an important role in deciding issues of medical ethics. It is notable that most religious views indicate a clear answer: an activity either is or is not permissible in God's eyes. Many writing from a non-religious perspective are far less sure there is a 'right answer' and tend to be more willing to allow practices if those involved consent.

■ Putting it all together

Answer guidelines

See the essay question at the start of the chapter.

Approaching the question

At first sight this is a rather intimidating question. You may worry that you don't know quite what the examiner is looking for. With such general questions in fact there are many good ways of answering them, and as long as you take a sensible approach the examiner will not mind how you go about it. You cannot be expected to cover every ethical approach in this question and so all you can do is select what you think are the main ones and discuss those.

Important points to include

A useful starting point in answering this question would be to go through the four key principles that Beauchamp and Childress (2012) have developed (as summarised above). You could then discuss whether these principles are useful. Do you agree that each case involves individuals and is different, and that it is not always possible to generate overarching principles that take account of all the different circumstances? Or is it useful for doctors to have general principles to apply so that they do not get caught up in the emotional and personal issues that are raised?

You can then turn to consider how clashes between these principles should be resolved. Do you think that autonomy should be the paramount principle? Are there any circumstances in which you think it appropriate to give a patient treatment against his or her wishes? Or, where it is inappropriate to give a treatment that a patient wishes to receive?

▶

✓ Make your answer stand out

It can make a really good impression if you apply these different theories to a
particular case. This will show that you can explain the theories in practice, but
also apply them in the real world.

READ TO IMPRESS

Beauchamp, T. and Childress, J. (2012) *Principles of Biomedical Ethics*. Oxford: Oxford University
Press.

Brazier, M. (2006) 'Do No Harm – Do Patients Have Responsibilities Too?', 65 *Cambridge Law
Journal* 397.

Foster, C. (2011) *Human Dignity in Bioethics and the Law*. Oxford: Hart.

Gillon, R. (2003) 'Ethics Needs Principles – Four Can Encompass the Rest – and Respect for
Autonomy Should Be "First Among Equals"', 29 *Journal of Medical Ethics* 307.

Harris, J. (ed.) (2001) *Bioethics*. Oxford: Oxford University Press.

Harris, J. (2003) 'In Praise of Unprincipled Ethics', 29 *Journal of Medial Ethics* 303.

Herring, J. (2007) 'Where Are the Carers in Healthcare Law and Ethics?', 27 *Legal Studies* 51.

Herring, J. (2012) *Medical Law and Ethics*. Oxford: Oxford University Press.

Holland, S. (2011) 'The Virtue Ethics Approach to Bioethics', 25 *Bioethics* 192.

Hope, T. (2005) *A Very Short Introduction to Medical Ethics*. Oxford: Oxford University Press.

Hursthouse, R. (1991) 'Virtue Theory and Abortion', 20 *Philosophy and Public Affairs* 223.

Kuhse, H. and Singer, P. (eds) (1998) *A Companion to Bioethics*. Oxford: Blackwell.

Pattinson, S. (2011) *Medical Law and Ethics*. London: Sweet and Maxwell.

Sheldon, S. and Thomson, M. (1998) *Feminist Perspectives on Health Care Law*. London:
Cavendish.

Tong, R. (1997) *Feminist Approaches to Bioethics: Theoretical Reflections and Practical
Applications*. Boulder, CO: Westview Press.

www.pearsoned.co.uk/lawexpress
Go online to access more revision support including quizzes to test your
knowledge, sample questions with answer guidelines, podcasts you can
download and more!

Rationing

2

Revision checklist

Essential points you should know:

- [ ] What rationing is
- [ ] How rationing decisions are made in the NHS
- [ ] How a rationing decision can be challenged in the courts
- [ ] The attitude of the courts towards rationing decisions
- [ ] The ethical issues surrounding rationing decisions

■ Topic map

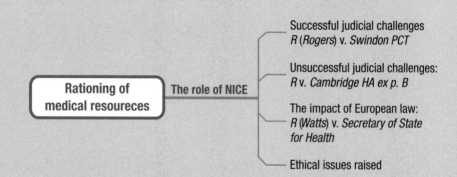

Rationing of medical resoureces — The role of NICE

Successful judicial challenges
R (Rogers) v. *Swindon PCT*

Unsuccessful judicial challenges:
R v. *Cambridge HA ex p. B*

The impact of European law:
R (Watts) v. *Secretary of State for Health*

Ethical issues raised

A printable version of this topic map is available from **www.pearsoned.co.uk/lawexpress**

■ Introduction

In an ideal world everyone would get the medical treatment they need.

However, it is generally agreed this is not possible, at least not without taxation at a higher level than it is currently. It would simply be too expensive to fund the treatment that everyone would like. Rationing decisions, therefore, need to be made to decide who will receive the limited resources available. In some cases rationing is not due to a lack of money, but a lack of other medical resources. An example is organ donation where there is a finite number of organs available for transplantation and simply not enough for everyone's need. The question of how to decide which treatments are available on the NHS and how to select which treatments a patient should receive is a highly controversial question. Not surprisingly, the courts, in recent years, have been drawn into the debates with legal challenges being brought over rationing decisions.

ASSESSMENT ADVICE

Essay questions

These require a good knowledge of the cases where rationing decisions have been challenged. There have not been too many of them and so you can be expected to know them well. You will need to discuss the work of the National Institute of Clinical Excellence (NICE). You should also address some of the issues which academics have debated:

- Should age be relevant in rationing decisions?
- Should it be relevant that patients have brought their condition upon themselves?
- How are we to assess who is in greatest need?

Problem questions

These are likely to ask you to consider what legal challenges could be made to a rationing decision. The case law will need to be used carefully in addressing the question. Note that, although several challenges have been successful, the courts are still generally reluctant to allow legal challenges. Anyone seeking to challenge a rationing decision will face an uphill battle. Do not exaggerate the significance of the cases and note how the judges have been careful to limit the impact of their decisions. A good answer will also raise the possible significance of the Human Rights Act to these decisions.

■ Sample question

Could you answer this question? Below is a typical problem question that could arise on this topic. Guidelines on answering the question are included at the end of this chapter, whilst a sample essay question and guidance on tackling it can be found on the companion website.

PROBLEM QUESTION

A new drug has been produced which its makers claim significantly reduces the risk of heart attack in cases of people with high cholesterol. NICE has announced it will be considering the drug in two years' time. Alf, Beatrice, Charlene and Dave have all been denied access to the drug by their local Primary Care Trust (PCT), but for different reasons.

In Alf's case, the PCT says it has a policy of never authorising new drugs until they have been approved by NICE.

In Beatrice's case, the PCT says there is inadequate clinical evidence that the drug is effective.

In Charlene's case, the PCT says it will supply the drug, but only to patients who are caring for children or elderly relatives. Charlene does not fall into this category.

In Dave's case, the PCT has said that it will not fund the drug if a patient's high cholesterol is due to their unhealthy diet because patients have only themselves to blame, and it prefers to fund blameless patients. Dave's cholesterol level is blamed on his penchant for eating very fatty foods and so he is denied the drug.

Discuss the chances of Alf, Beatrice, Charlene and Dave in challenging the decisions of their PCTs in a court.

■ Rationing

Most people accept that the National Health Service cannot provide every patient with every treatment they may want. There is simply not enough money within the NHS to provide every treatment that is needed. This means decisions have to be made as to which patient can receive which treatment.

KEY DEFINITION: Rationing

Where there is only a limited healthcare resource and a decision must be made to offer the resources to some patients and not others.

✓ Make your answer stand out

A really good answer on rationing will point out that we do not need to assume that rationing must take place. Although funding all treatment that is needed on the NHS would require an increase in taxation (or drastic cuts elsewhere), the increase might not be more than a few percentage points. If politicians were open with the public and said that either life-saving treatments would not be available on the NHS or income tax would have to increase by a few percentage points, are we sure that the public would rather keep low taxes? Indeed, should we simply decide that, morally speaking, society is obliged to provide for the healthcare needs of its citizens? If that requires an increase in taxation, that must occur.

It is important to appreciate that rationing can occur at a number of levels within the NHS:

- The government must decide how much money to allocate to health rather than other needs (e.g. transport).
- Decisions are made as to how to divide up the health budget among the different bodies and organisations within the NHS.
- A local body may decide how to allocate its budget to meet the needs of people in its area.
- A doctor may decide whether or not a particular treatment is cost-effective.

■ The role of NICE

The National Institute for Health and Clinical Excellence (NICE) plays an important role in rationing decisions. It has the job of advising on the clinical effectiveness of drugs and their value for money. Although its guidance is not officially binding on PCTs, it should be followed. Part of the aim in creating NICE was that there would be consistent approaches to controversial treatments across the NHS. This would avoid the so-called 'postcode lottery', where patients in some parts of the country have access to treatment, but in other parts do not. In making its decisions, NICE pays much attention to the **quality adjusted life years** (QALY) value of treatment.

KEY DEFINITION: Quality adjusted life year

This is an assessment of the benefit of a treatment. It takes into account how many years' extra life a treatment may provide and the increase in the quality of life that a treatment may provide.

NICE will consider how many QALYs a treatment will provide and at what cost. This provides a way of comparing treatments for the same medical condition. It also provides a way of comparing treatments for completely different medical conditions. If one treatment offers many years of greatly improved quality of life, it will be preferred over a treatment which will offer only a few years of low-quality life. It also enables NICE to consider the costs of different treatments. So a treatment which offers many QALYs at a low price is almost bound to be approved by NICE.

✓ **Make your answer stand out**

Although QALYs are widely used in the NHS, an excellent answer will consider whether they are justifiable. The use of QALYs is controversial. Is it possible to value quality of life? Is it worse being confined to a wheelchair or being blind? Do we want to start putting figures on such things? Others argue that it works against the interests of older people and those with a disability. This is because they may not be able to show as much gain from the treatment, or for as long a time, as a young person in generally good health. Harris (2005) argues that all patients who require a particular treatment should be entitled to it on the basis of the principle of equality. Further controversy surrounds whether the benefits to those who care for patients should be considered when assessing the gains from the treatment (Herring (2007)), or whether the fact that a patient is at fault in needing the treatment should be relevant (i.e. should we prefer the victim of lung cancer who has endured passive smoke over the smoker?)

✎ **EXAM TIP**

In an essay question it is a good idea to discuss the role of NICE. To cynics, NICE was created so that the making of unpalatable decisions on who would or would not receive treatment would be taken by an organisation which is independent of government. In other words, it was a way of deflecting blame from politicians. Other commentators think that it was sensible to place the decision with an organisation which is free from political pressure and makes decisions which are based on objective facts, rather than which group of patients has the best pressure group or can garner the most public sympathy. The relationship between NICE and the government has been uneasy, with, in one case, a government minister appearing to overrule a decision by NICE on breast cancer treatment. There are certainly dangers that, if politicians do start to interfere in decisions made by NICE, the organisation will be more widely seen as a smokescreen. Currently, it appears to have a generally good reputation for making independent judgements. For further discussion, see Syrett (2002).

■ Judicial challenges to rationing decisions

If a patient wishes to take his or her PCT to court for failing to provide treatment, this is most likely to be done by means of judicial review. It is necessary to show that the decision reached was irrational. Such claims have rarely succeeded because the courts have recognised that healthcare bodies often face difficult decisions. The court is not in a position to weigh up all the competing claims that they have on their resources. Although the court will know of the case before it, it will not know the details of all the other cases that the PCT has to deal with. As the following case shows, this point is taken even where the needs of the patient appear compelling.

KEY CASE

R v. Cambridge Health Authority ex p. B [1995] 1 WLR 898
Concerning: whether 'life-saving' treatment could be denied

Facts

Jaymee Bowen, aged 10, was suffering from acute myeloid leukaemia. The doctors treating her agreed that the only possible treatment (intense chemotherapy and a bone marrow transplant) was very unlikely to succeed and would be very painful. Her father found a doctor in London who was willing to provide the treatment, but he could not afford the private fees. He sought an order that Cambridge HA pay for the treatment.

Legal principle

The Court of Appeal held that health authorities had to make difficult decisions about how to spend their money. They cannot provide all the treatment they would like. The court cannot require the health authority to justify its resource allocations. In this case the court had to respect the decision of the health authority that this was not treatment which it was appropriate to spend its money on.

✎ EXAM TIP

When discussing *R v. Cambridge ex p. B* it is useful to contrast the approach of Laws J at first instance with that of the Court of Appeal. Laws J emphasised Jaymee's human rights. He said that the health authority had to 'do more than toll the bell of tight resources'. The HA had to explain precisely how its priorities had led it to deny life-saving treatment. The court would need to be satisfied that the interference in the patient's human rights to life-saving treatment was justified. The Court of Appeal felt it was not the job of the court to determine how well a HA distributed its limited resources.

The courts, when hearing claims that a rationing policy has treated a patient unfairly are all too aware of the need to balance the interests of the individual patient with those of the wider community.

KEY CASE

R (Condliff) v. *North Staffordshire PCT* [2011] EWHC 895 (Admin)

Concerning: challenge to rationing treatment

Facts

Mr Condliff was morbidly obese and wished to have bariatric surgery. Although he did not qualify under the Trust's policy, he argued that he was an exceptional case given the impact of his obesity on his lifestyle and happiness. The Trust's policy did not allow consideration of lifestyle factors and so his application was refused.

Legal principle

Mr Cuncliffe's claim that his rights under Article 8 of the ECHR were breached because the Trust refused to consider social factors was rejected. There had to be a fair balancing between the individuals claiming exceptional circumstances and the medical needs of a community as a whole. The Trust had adopted a reasonable policy and so Mr Cuncliffe's claim failed.

■ Cases where judicial challenges have been successful

Where the health authority has taken a rigid approach which fails to properly take into account each particular individual, this is particularly susceptible to challenge. That is demonstrated by the following cases.

KEY CASE

R v. *North West Lancashire Health Authority ex p. A* [2000] 1 WLR 977

Concerning: denying gender reassignment surgery

Facts

The applicants suffered gender identity dysphoria. Two of them were found to have a clinical need for gender reassignment surgery (colloquially, a 'sex change' operation). The health authority decided that it would not pay for such surgery because it was unclear whether the surgery would be helpful. However, in exceptional cases, the Director of Public Health could authorise funding.

Legal principle

In effect, the policy was a blanket ban on funding the surgery. It was not really imagined that the Director would ever authorise funding in cases of this kind. This meant that individual cases were not considered on their own merits. The approach taken by the HA was, therefore, unlawful. Further, the HA had failed to acknowledge that transsexualism was a medical condition for which the surgery was a recognised treatment.

In the following case it appears to have been the reluctance of the PCT to admit that the decisions were being made on the basis of economics which caused the court problems. A health authority should be open and clear about what its policy is and how it operates. Otherwise, there is a danger it will be successfully challenged in the courts.

KEY CASE

R (Rogers) v. *Swindon NHS Primary Health Care Trust* [2006] EWCA Civ 392
Concerning: rationing drugs for breast cancer

Facts

Swindon Primary Health Care Trust refused to fund Ms Rogers's treatment with Herceptin for breast cancer. Although her consultant had recommended that she use the drug, the PCT had a policy of only funding it in 'exceptional cases' and found that hers was not exceptional. She sought judicial review of the PCT's decision.

Legal principle

If a PCT decides that monetary considerations are not an issue, then all patients who clinically need a particular drug should be given it. There were no clinical or personal reasons that could justify giving the drug to some patients and not others among the group of those for whom the drug was clinically appropriate. A policy of allowing drugs to be given in 'exceptional' cases could only be lawful if it was clear what those exceptional circumstances might be.

Although judicial review challenges to rationing decisions are normally brought against the PCT, it would be possible to seek judicial review of a ruling by NICE. In *R (Eisai)* v. *National Institute for Health and Clinical Excellence* (2008) the Court of Appeal allowed a judicial review challenge to a decision made by NICE, because it had failed to be sufficiently open about its procedures.

✎ EXAM TIP

A good point to make in the exam is that the courts tend to be reluctant to overturn a rationing decision on the basis simply that the decision was wrong. Although it may be willing to do so if the PCT has made an error of fact (e.g. the approach to transsexualism in the *R* v. *NW Lancashire HA ex p. A* (2000) case), the courts will be more willing to intervene if they are persuaded that the decision-making process is flawed. This might be where a blanket policy is pursued, without considering each case individually, or the real reasons behind a decision not being made open (e.g. where the decision is really made on the basis of financial considerations, but the PCT says it is a clinical decision).

It may be that in the future the most profitable line of claim will be that a particular policy was discriminatory. In *R (AC)* v. *West Primary Care Trust* (2011) a trans woman who was denied breast augmentation surgery, under the policy that applied to all people seeking breast augmentation, failed in a claim that the policy discriminated against her. Under the Equality Act 2010 and the NHS Constitution, age discrimination is prohibited and so future cases may raise that issue.

The impact of European Union law

In the following case the potential significance of European Union law was considered. At the heart of the claim is Article 49 of the EC Treaty which allows freedom to provide services within the community. The European Court of Justice has held that services include medical treatment. The question in this case was whether an NHS patient who could not get treatment within a reasonable length of time from the NHS had the right to travel to another EC country for that treatment and then claim recompense from the NHS for the costs.

KEY CASE

R (Watts) v. *Secretary of State for Health* [2004] EWCA Civ 166

Concerning: whether the NHS could be required to pay for medical treatment received by British citizens in other EU states

Facts

Ms Watts needed a hip transplant. When she was told that this would take over a year under the NHS, she travelled to France and had the operation there. She claimed that under Article 49 of the EC Treaty and Council Regulation 1408/71, Article 22 the NHS had to pay for the treatment.

Legal principle

The English Court of Appeal held that the NHS was not liable to pay. Article 49 did not apply to state-funded healthcare systems. Article 22 did not apply where the delay was caused by economic circumstances.

The European Court of Justice disagreed. It held that patients could rely on Articles 49 and 22 to claim expenses. In future, where a NHS patient is facing medically unacceptable waiting times, the patient can seek prior authorisation for funding. Any decision will take into account the patient's medical condition and the degree of pain and disability.

The *Watts* decision has been controversial. Supporters say that it means that EU citizens should be entitled to a reasonable standard of healthcare and that if that cannot be provided in their own country, they must be free to receive it in another country. Opponents are concerned that *Watts* will only help middle-class patients who will have the resources to find hospitals in Europe which can treat them and make the appropriate applications to the PCT. Note there is no requirement on a PCT to find an overseas hospital to provide treatment if its waiting lists become unacceptably long.

■ Putting it all together

Answer guidelines

See the essay question at the start of the chapter.

Approaching the question

You will need to consider each of the four people separately. There may be some general principles which apply for all cases and you could start with them, before looking at each case. You will want to make sure you show a good knowledge of the case law.

Important points to include

You should start by emphasising how hard it is to succeed in challenging a rationing decision. In order to show that the decision has been unreasonable, it has to be shown that the approach taken is so unreasonable that no reasonable healthcare body could have made it.

In Alf's case, you will want to make the point that the courts tend to disapprove of strict approaches that fail to take account of each individual case. Notice also that NICE is only meant to offer guidance to a PCT, albeit guidance that it is expected it should follow. A PCT cannot delegate its responsibilities to NICE.

In Beatrice's case, the challenge is likely to prove difficult. As *ex p. B* shows, the courts are reluctant to challenge an assessment that a treatment is ineffective, unless it can be shown that there is a clear flaw in the reasoning used.

In Charlene's case, the *Rogers* case should be referred to. It may be argued that this is too restrictive on what will count as an exceptional case (there is no reference to disabled adults who are not elderly). Article 14 of the ECHR could be used if the policy is seen to discriminate on the basis of disability.

In Dave's case, the *Rogers* decision suggests that such personal characteristics should not be relied upon. See also the NICE (2006) guidance on this.

> ✓ **Make your answer stand out**
>
> It would be good to mention the Equality Act 2010 which has recently forbidden unjustified discrimination by public bodies. This is particularly relevant in Charlene's case. Bring in as much of the recent case law as you can to capture the current approach of the courts.

READ TO IMPRESS

Bærøe, K. and Bringedal, B. (2011) 'Just Health: on the conditions for acceptable and unacceptable priority settings with respect to patients' socioeconomic status', 37 *Journal of Medical Ethics* 526.

Ford, A. (2012) 'The Concept of Exceptionality: A legal farce', 20(3) *Medical Law Review* 304.

Golan, O. (2010) 'The Right to Treatment for Self-inflicted Conditions', 36 *Journal of Medical Ethics* 683.

Harris, J. (2005) 'It's Not NICE to Discriminate', 31 *Journal of Medical Ethics* 373.

Herring, J. (2007) 'Where are the Carers in Healthcare Law and Ethics?', 27 *Legal Studies* 51.

Newdick, C. (2005) *Who Shall We Treat?* Oxford: Oxford University Press.

NICE (2006) *Social Value Judgements*. London: NICE.

Syrett, K. (2002) 'NICE Work? Rationing, Review and the "Legitimacy Problem" in the New NHS', 10 *Medical Law Review* 1.

Syrett, K. (2004) 'Impotence or Importance? Judicial Review in an Era of Explicit NHS Rationing', 67 *Modern Law Review* 289.

www.pearsoned.co.uk/lawexpress

Go online to access more revision support including quizzes to test your knowledge, sample questions with answer guidelines, podcasts you can download, and more!

Consent to treatment

3

■ Topic map

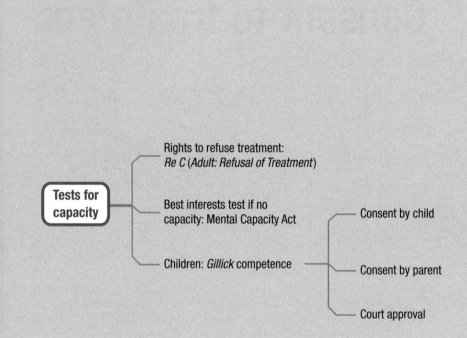

Tests for capacity
- Rights to refuse treatment: *Re C (Adult: Refusal of Treatment)*
- Best interests test if no capacity: Mental Capacity Act
- Children: *Gillick* competence
  - Consent by child
  - Consent by parent
  - Court approval

A printable version of this topic map is available from **www.pearsoned.co.uk/lawexpress**

■ Introduction

A doctor can only provide treatment to a competent patient with that patient's consent.

This apparently simple proposition is, in fact, far more complicated than at first appears. First, there is the question of what it means for a patient to be competent. Second, there is the question of how much information a patient must be given in order to be able to make an effective decision. Third, there is the question of how patients who lack capacity should be treated.

ASSESSMENT ADVICE

Essay questions

The questions on this topic will require a good knowledge of not only the legal principles, but also the ethical ones. You will need a detailed knowledge of the Mental Capacity Act 2005 and to be able to explain how the courts will assess capacity and how decisions are made on behalf of those who lack capacity. You may also be asked to discuss how seriously the law takes the rights of patients to make decisions about their treatment. Here you would need to consider not only what the courts say they are doing, but also the actual results in the cases. Some academics (e.g. Harrington (1996)) are suspicious that the courts find a patient to lack capacity if they think the patient's decision unwise. Another topical issue which could appear in an essay question is how much information a patient should be given. The notion of 'informed consent' has received much attention from the courts and academics. On the ethical principles, you will need to explain the principle of autonomy and how it is seen as such an important principle. But you need also to be able to discuss the concerns about overemphasising autonomy and objections to the principle.

Problem questions

These are likely to require you to discuss a number of issues raised by this chapter. There may well be some debate over whether a patient lacks capacity or not. There may also be a discussion about what decision should be made if they do, indeed, lack capacity. In answering these, the Mental Capacity Act 2005 now governs the law and there is little case law discussing the new legislation. However, you can use earlier case law as a guide to indicate how the Act might be interpreted. The problem question may also raise questions about an advance decision. Note, in particular, that generally an advance decision does not need to be in writing, but it does if it involves the refusal of life-saving treatment.

■ Sample question

Could you answer this question? Below is a typical problem question that could arise on this topic. Guidelines on answering the question are included at the end of this chapter, whilst a sample essay question and guidance on tackling it can be found on the companion website.

PROBLEM QUESTION

Angelina is aged 25 and has been badly injured in a car crash. Doctors wish to use a new treatment which has been developed following embryo research, without which it is very likely she will die. Angelina has been seen by a psychologist who explains that she is aware that she is very ill, but is finding it very difficult to concentrate because she is in great pain. The psychologist says that Angelina is not in a position to understand the exact nature of the treatment she is being offered, or the risks associated with it. She is, however, aware that the treatment could save her life. Angelina says that she does not want the treatment and she wants to die. Before the accident, Angelina had been completing a doctorate in medical law. The doctorate was arguing strongly against the use of medical treatments developed using embryo research. Angelina was a member of her local church and her pastor says that her church believes that people should never refuse life-saving treatment. The pastor is adamant that Angelina would have wanted the treatment. Angelina's boyfriend is also confident that she would have wanted the treatment. Angelina's mother is opposed to her being given any treatment. There is a note in Angelina's diary which says that if she is ever ill, everything should be done to save her life.

Discuss what treatment, if any, the doctors may administer to Angela.

■ The basic approach of the law

A key principle in medical law is that competent patients have the right to refuse treatment. 'Doctors know best' may or may not be true, but if a competent patient has not consented to the treatment, the doctor cannot force it on them. This is true, as the following case shows, even if some might regard the patient's decision as bizarre.

KEY CASE

Re C (Adult: Refusal of Treatment) [1994] 1 WLR 290
Concerning: whether a competent adult has the right to refuse treatment

Facts

C had been diagnosed as suffering from paranoid schizophrenia and was a patient at Broadmoor. One of his delusional beliefs was that he was a great doctor. He was diagnosed with gangrene in his foot. He was told he needed to have an amputation of the foot without which he would die. C accepted that that was the doctors' view but disagreed with them. In any event, he believed God would heal him. He refused to consent to treatment. The doctors sought permission to amputate the foot.

Legal principle

Thorpe J held that C was competent. He understood what the doctors were saying to him. He understood that they believed he would die without the treatment. He was able to reach the clear decision of his own to reject their opinions. Patients should not be found incompetent simply because they do not agree with medical opinion or their decision is regarded by others as irrational. The doctors were therefore not allowed to operate on him without his consent. (It later transpired that his foot made a remarkable recovery!)

The principle in this case is reflected in the Mental Capacity Act 2005.

KEY STATUTE

Mental Capacity Act 2005, section 1(3)

A person is not to be treated as unable to make a decision merely because he makes an unwise decision.

❗ Don't be tempted to . . .

Some students make the mistake of assuming that a patient should be found to be incompetent simply because a decision they have made is unwise. The Mental Capacity Act 2005 makes it clear that is an impermissible line of reasoning. Nevertheless, some academics have argued that, in fact, the courts have given way in some cases to deeming a patient incompetent because the judge believes that the decision reached is absurd (e.g. Harrington (1996)). Of course, an obvious sign that a person lacks competence is the making of absurd decisions. On the other hand, a proper respect for autonomy must give effect to mistaken decisions or else it does not mean very much. If the law only respected your decisions if doctors thought they were sensible it would not really be respecting your choice. There are ethical debates to be had here, too. If a person's thinking is illogical and contradicts other values which are important to them, does it actually promote their autonomy to follow their decision?

■ What is consent?

In order for a patient to give effective consent, it is not enough just that the patient says 'yes'; it must be shown that:

- the patient is competent
- the patient is sufficiently informed
- the patient is not subject to coercion or undue influence
- the patient has reached a clear decision.

Competence

The test for competence is set out in the Mental Capacity Act 2005. The starting point is that person is presumed competent unless it is shown that they lack capacity. The two key provisions on capacity are as follows.

KEY STATUTE

Mental Capacity Act 2005, sections 2(1) and 3(1)

2 (1) . . . A person lacks capacity in relation to a matter if at the material time he is unable to make a decision for himself in relation to the matter because of an impairment of, or a disturbance in the functioning of, the mind or brain.

3 (1) For the purposes of section 2, a person is unable to make a decision for himself if he is unable –

(a) to understand the information relevant to the decision,

(b) to retain that information,

(c) to use or weigh that information as part of the process of making the decision, or

(d) to communicate his decision (whether by talking, using sign language or any other means).

✎ EXAM TIP

An important point to make in an exam is that the Act focuses on potential capacity as well as actual capacity. Even if a patient lacks capacity at the moment, if the patient can be helped to become competent, then they may not lack capacity. The Act, for example, requires that patients be given the information they need to make a decision in an appropriate form (e.g. through sign language).

> ## ! Don't be tempted to . . .
>
> It would be wrong to think that a person is treated as generally lacking capacity. The law recognises that a person may have capacity to make some decisions, but not others. For example, a person may have capacity to decide where they want to go on holiday, but not have the capacity to sign a will. All will depend on what facts they are able to understand.

A good example of the law on capacity is the following case.

KEY CASE

A Local Authority v. *Mrs A and Mr A* [2010] EWHC 1549 (Fam)

Concerning: the test for capacity

Facts

Mrs A had low intellectual functioning and had two children taken into care as she did not understand how to care for them. After that she had been receiving a monthly contraceptive injection. However, she then married Mr A and stopped taking the injection, explaining that Mr A did not want her to.

Legal principle

Mrs A had sufficient understanding to make the decision about contraception because she understood the central issue (i.e. what contraception did) even though she did not understand the broader issue (e.g. what raising a child would be like). However, because she was in an abusive relationship, she did not have the freedom to make the decision. Using the best interests test, it was decided not to force her to have the contraception because that would not be in her best interests.

Information

A patient will be treated as sufficiently informed to make a decision if they understand in broad terms the nature of the proposed treatment (*Chatterton* v. *Gerson* (1981)). A patient, therefore, can consent even if they have not been informed of all of the risks of an operation. However, where a person is unaware of a crucial fact about the treatment, there will not be effective consent. So, where a man gave a woman a breast examination claiming falsely to be medically qualified, it was held that she had not consented to the 'treatment' (*R* v. *Tabassum* (2000)).

3 CONSENT TO TREATMENT

✎ **EXAM TIP**

Where a patient has not been given an important piece of information before consenting to a medical procedure, there are two legal complaints the patient could make. First, that the lack of information means the consent was not legally effective and so the doctor has committed the tort of battery and possibly a crime. Second, that it was negligent for the doctor not to provide the information. The first rarely arises because it is unlikely that a patient would not understand in broad terms what the treatment was. The second may be more common, but it can be difficult then to show what loss was caused by the negligence, at least where the medical operation goes well.

The patient must be free from undue influence

A patient can only provide an effective consent if acting free from coercion or undue influence. So if it is felt that a patient is acting under pressure from, for example, a parent, then the consent will be invalid (*Re T (Adult: Refusal of Treatment)* (1992); *A Local Authority v. Mrs A and Mr A* (2010)). A patient may also be found to be so exhausted or in so much pain as to lack capacity (*NHS Trust v. T* (2004)).

Consent to what?

Sometimes, although it is clear that the patient has consented to some medical treatment, there is a dispute over which medical treatment they consented to. A court will readily accept, that if there is consent to an operation, there is also consent to the procedures necessary if the operation is to go ahead (e.g. the giving of anaesthetic). However, the law is also clear that giving consent to one operation is not consent to any operation!

■ Cases of negligence

Where a doctor has failed to provide information about the risks of an operation, as well as claiming that there was no consent to the operation, another potential claim is that the doctor behaved negligently. The problem, however, is in showing what loss the patient suffered as a result of the negligence, especially if the operation was a success! The following cases are very useful.

KEY CASE

***Sidaway* v. *Bethlem Royal Hospital Governors* [1985] 1 All ER 643**
Concerning: how much information should be given to a patient

Facts

Mrs Sidaway claimed that she was not warned about the risks of an operation to relieve a trapped nerve. The operation had left her paralysed. She sued in negligence on the basis that she had not been properly given the necessary information to consent effectively to it.

Legal principle

Each of the judges in the House of Lords provided a slightly different explanation. Lord Diplock thought the case should rely on the *Bolam* test (see Chapter 5). As there was a respectable body of opinion that found it acceptable not to warn patients of the risks in an operation of this kind, the doctor could not be found to be negligent. Lords Bridge and Keith agreed with the use of the *Bolam* test, but indicated that a judge may be willing to find that even if there was a body of medical opinion saying that a risk should not be disclosed, it may well not be respectable. Lord Templeman thought that doctors were only required to reveal general risks attached to an operation if they were asked about them by a patient. Lord Scarman suggested a doctor could rightly decide that warning a patient of a risk would cause such distress to the patient that it should not be done.

KEY CASE

Chester v. *Afshar* [2004] UKHL 41

Concerning: when a doctor was liable for failing to warn of a risk

Facts

Ms Chester suffered back pain. Her consultant, Mr Afshar, recommended surgery but failed to warn her of the one to two per cent chance of severe nerve damage. The operation was performed properly but nerve damage resulted and she was partially paralysed. The court found that if Ms Chester had been warned of the operation, she would have eventually agreed to the operation, but at a later time, having sought further advice.

Legal principle

Ms Chester was entitled to damages. Had she been made aware of the risk, she would not have consented to have the operation at the time she did. It was true that she would have consented to the operation later and it would have carried the same risks as the operation she, in fact, had. Nevertheless, there was a sufficient causal link between the negligence of Dr Afshar and the injuries suffered by Ms Chester. In part their Lordships emphasised that doctors should warn patients of the risks that medical procedures carried. They should not be able to breach those duties and then escape liability in tort.

■ If a competent patient does not consent, is it ever permissible still to administer treatment?

The short answer is 'No'! But that would not be 100 per cent accurate. There are a few circumstances where it might. Under the 1988 Public Health (Infectious Diseases) Regulations, a magistrate can order a person suffering from a 'notifiable disease' (e.g. cholera) to be detained for treatment. Although the law is not completely clear, it appears that it is also lawful to use medical treatment to prevent a person from committing suicide (*R* v. *Collins and Ashworth Hospital Authority ex p. Brady* (2000)). A more representative case of the current law would be *St George's Healthcare NHS Trust* v. *S* where it was found to be unlawful to perform a Caesarean section operation on a woman who did not consent to it, even though without it she and her baby would die.

In the last few years the courts have developed a jurisdiction to deal with vulnerable adults. These are adults who do have capacity, but only just, and are regarded as vulnerable. So far, most of the cases have involved disputes over where the vulnerable adult should live (e.g. *Dorset CC* v. *EH* (2009); *DL* v. *A Local Authority* (2012)); but it may be that in the future it will be used in medical cases.

✓ Make your answer stand out

It is worth thinking further about the principle of autonomy. Is it right that a patient has an absolute right to refuse treatment? What if a patient had an unusual DNA which could provide a cure for cancer, should they be entitled to refuse to have a sample of their hair removed? Or what of a patient who refuses treatment and, as a result, the burden falling on their family is much greater than would be otherwise? See Harrington (1996).

■ The treatment of incompetent adults

So, if a patient is incompetent, how are medical decisions to be made? There are two key questions. First, who makes the decision? Second, on what basis are the decisions to be made?

Who decides?

The Mental Capacity Act 2005 states how to determine who will make the decision on behalf of an incompetent person. It is whoever is highest up the following list:

- the patient, if their wishes are clear in an advance decision, made while the patient had capacity
- a person appointed by the patient as having a lasting power of attorney
- the deputy appointed by the court.

If none of these exists, is it best to apply to the court for the appointment of a deputy? Failing that, a medical-health professional can treat patients in a way which most promotes their best interests. Notice that if there is an effective **advance decision** stating that a patient does not want to receive treatment, a doctor should not provide it.

KEY DEFINITION: Advance decision

An advance decision is a decision made by a patient about the treatment they wished to receive, or not to receive, if they lost capacity. It must have been made when the patient was over 18 and had capacity. The advance decision only becomes effective when the patient loses capacity.

KEY STATUTE

Mental Capacity Act 2005, section 26(1)

If P [the patient] has made an advance decision which is –

(a) valid, and

(b) applicable to the treatment,

the decision has the effect as if he had made it, and had had capacity to make it, at the time when the question arises whether the treatment should be carried out or continued.

REVISION NOTE

There are special rules regarding advance decisions to refuse life-saving treatment (see Chapter 9). These need to be in writing, signed and witnessed.

EXAM TIP

You must appreciate that the advance decision only applies to refusals of treatment. You cannot through an advance direction demand that you be given treatment. Although, of course, when deciding whether it would be in a patient's best interests to give a particular treatment, the fact that a patient has explicitly stated in advance to want it will be a relevant factor. The ethics of advance directives are also complex. Is it right that individuals at one point in time can determine what treatment they will receive at a later point in time (see Dresser (1994))? Is it possible for someone to know what they will want when later becoming incompetent? Or do advance directives provide a way of helping people keep control of their lives, even when they lose capacity?

How are decisions to be made on behalf of an incompetent person?

This is (at first) an easy question. The answer is that the decision must be made based on what is in the best interests of the person. But that is much easier to say than to put into practice. The Mental Capacity Act 2005 gives some guidance on what factors may be taken into account in determining what is in a patient's best interests.

KEY STATUTE

Mental Capacity Act 2005, section 4(6)

(a) the person's past and present wishes and feelings (and, in particular, any relevant written statement made by him when he had capacity),

(b) the beliefs and values that would be likely to influence his decision if he had capacity, and

(c) the other factors that he would be likely to consider if he were able to do so.

! Don't be tempted to . . .

In some jurisdictions the law uses the doctrine of 'substituted judgement'. English law does not use that doctrine and so make sure you make it clear in your essays that it is not part of the law. Under the doctrine of substituted judgement, the decision-maker must make the decision for the incompetent person based on what they think the person would have decided if the person had been competent. This will often be the same as asking what is in their best interests, but not always. It may be, for example, that the person had a religious objection to a treatment which would be in their best medical interests. Note that under the Mental Capacity Act 2005, in deciding what is in a person's best interests, the courts are required to consider the beliefs of the person, but it is unclear how much weight should be given to them. It seems that a person's previous beliefs cannot be used to justify treating them in a way which is clearly harmful. In *A London Local Authority* v. *JH* (2011) it was stated that the current views of the person lacking capacity were a factor to be taken into account when deciding what was in a person's best interests, but only one factor, and a court could determine that what the person wanted was not in their best interests.

The Mental Capacity Act 2005 makes it clear that the decision must be made based on what is best for the patient who lacks capacity. The decision should not be made just because that is what is most convenient for the individual's family or those looking after them. However, it is not always easy to separate out the interests of patients and their families, as the following case shows.

Re Y (Mental Incapacity: Bone Marrow Transplant) [1997] 2 FCR 172

Concerning: whether bone marrow could be taken from a patient lacking capacity

Facts

Y was severely mentally handicapped. She lived in a community home, but was regularly visited by her mother. Y's sister suffered a bone disorder. The only real chance of recovery was if bone marrow was taken from Y and given to the sister. The court was asked to authorise the harvesting of the bone marrow.

Legal principle

The procedure was lawful because it would be in Y's best interests. Y did not have a close relationship with her sister. However, if the sister were to fall more seriously ill and die, this would affect the mother's ability to visit Y and care for her. For Y it was important that her visits with her mother continued successfully. The harvesting would be only a 'minimal detriment' to Y. It was, therefore, in Y's best interests.

Where an adult who lacks capacity is being deprived of their liberty, then there are special safeguards (known as Deprivation of Liberty Safeguards) which apply. These are found in the Mental Capacity Act 2005, section 4 and Schedule A1. These set out the requirements which must be satisfied before a person can be deprived of their liberty and require that the deprivation be proportionate to the risk they are facing and be justified in their best interests.

■ Medical treatment of children

A child is a person under the age of 18. In order to treat a child, a doctor needs effective consent. This can be provided by any of the following:

- a child aged 16 or 17
- a *Gillick* competent child (see below)
- a person with parental responsibility for the child
- an order of the court.

If the case is a medical emergency and it not possible to obtain one of these consents, then a doctor may have a defence under the doctrine of necessity.

KEY DEFINITION: A *Gillick* competent child

A child who has sufficient maturity and understanding to make a competent decision about the issue. The child will need to understand not only the medical issues involved, but also the moral and family questions.

Notice, that although a competent child can effectively consent to treatment, if the child refuses, a parent can still consent on the child's behalf. Indeed, even if the child and their parents refuse to consent to the treatment, the court can still authorise it. The courts have done this in cases where children and parents belong to the Jehovah's Witnesses religious group and refuse to consent to the child receiving a life-saving blood transfusion (e.g. *Re E (A Minor)* (1993)).

✔ Make your answer stand out

The current state of the law in relation to children is controversial and there is much to discuss. A good essay will consider some of the following points. In effect, the courts have said that a competent child has the right to say 'yes' but not the right to say 'no'. This is because even if the child refuses treatment, unlike an adult, consent can be provided by someone else. Some commentators argue that if the child is as competent as an adult, they should be treated in law as an adult. Others argue that the current law is based not on protecting the rights of children, but ensuring that they receive their medical needs. Also debated are the cases where the courts have overridden the views of children and parents. Do the courts know better than parents what is good for their children? On the other hand, should parents be allowed to martyr their children? (See Herring (2007) for a discussion of these issues.) Also note that only one parent has to consent. In *An NHS Trust* v. *SR* (2012) the mother refused to consent to treatment, but the father did consent. The court held it was permissible for the hospital to provide the treatment as they had consent from a parent.

■ Putting it all together

Answer guidelines

See the problem question at the start of the chapter.

Approaching the question

This problem question raises quite a number of issues and it is important to have a clear structure. Use one paragraph to discuss each issue separately. You will need to keep the best interests test central to the answer.

Important points to include

The first issue here is to determine whether or not Angelina is competent to make a decision over her treatment. You will want to refer to the test for capacity in the Mental Capacity Act 2005. Note that it needs to be shown that she is able to understand the issues and able to reach a decision (*A Local Authority* v. *Mrs A and Mr A* (2010)).

If she is found competent, remember that she has an absolute right to refuse treatment. Refer to the case law on this (e.g. *St George's Healthcare NHS Trust* v. *S* (1998)).

If she is found incompetent, you will need to determine who can make the decision on Angelina's behalf. You will need to consider whether or not there has been an advance decision in this case, based on what is in the diary. If this is ineffective, who is the nearest relative?

Whoever the decision-maker is, they must make the decision based on what is in Angelina's best interests. Note that although the decision-maker may take into account her religious and other views, ultimately, it is a question about what is in her best interests. Note that if anyone disagrees with the decision-maker, the matter can be brought to court for a judge to rule on what is in her best interests.

> ✓ **Make your answer stand out**
>
> Make sure you make the fine distinction between an advance decision, which if binding, will determine the case; and a previous expression of views which is only a factor to be taken into account in determining best interests.

READ TO IMPRESS

Coggon, J. and Miola, J. (2011) 'Autonomy, Liberty and Medical Decision-making', 70(3) *Cambridge Law Journal* 523.

Donnelly, M. (2009) 'Capacity Assessment under the Mental Capacity Act 2005: delivering on the function approach', 29 *Legal Studies* 464.

Donnelly, M. (2010) 'Determining Best Interests under The Mental Capacity Act 2005', 19 *Medical Law Review* 27.

Dresser, R. (1994) 'Missing Persons: legal perceptions of incompetent patients', 46 *Rutgers Law Review* 609.

Foster, C. (2009) *Choosing Life, Choosing Death.* Oxford: Hart.

Gilmore, S. and Herring, J. (2011) '"No" is the Hardest Word: consent and children's autonomy', 23 *Child and Family Law Quarterly* 3.

GMC (2008) *Consent: Patients and Doctors Making Decisions Together*, London: GMC.

Harrington, J. (1996) 'Privileging the Medical Norm: liberalism, self-determination and refusal of treatment', 16 *Legal Studies* 348.

Herring, J. (2010) 'Losing it? Losing What? The Law and Dementia', 21 *Child and Family Law Quarterly* 3.

Herring, J. (2010) *Family Law*. Harlow: Pearson.

Herring, J. and Foster, C. (2012) 'Welfare Means Relationality, Virtue and Altruism', 32 *Legal Studies* 480.

Lewis, P. (2002) 'Procedures that are Against the Medical Interests of the Incompetent Person', 12 *Oxford Journal of Legal Studies* 12.

Maclean, A. (2004) 'The Doctrine of Informed Consent: does it exist and has it crossed the Atlantic?', 24 *Legal Studies* 386.

Maclean, A. (2008) 'Advance Directives and the Rocky Waters of Anticipatory Decision-making', 16 *Medical Law Review* 1.

Maclean, A. (2009) *Autonomy, Informed Consent and the Law: A Relational Challenge*. Cambridge: Cambridge University Press.

www.pearsoned.co.uk/lawexpress

Go online to access more revision support including quizzes to test your knowledge, sample questions with answer guidelines, podcasts you can download, and more!

Confidentiality

4

Revision checklist

Essential points you should know:

- [ ] The legal basis of confidentiality
- [ ] When it is permissible to breach confidence
- [ ] The issues surrounding the confidentiality of genetic information
- [ ] What rights there are to access your medical records

Topic map

Legal basis for protecting confidential information
- Breach of contract
- Equitable breach of confidence
  - Personal information: *Campbell* v. *MGN*
  - Circumstance of confidence
  - Unauthorised disclosure
  - No justification: *W* v. *Edgell*
- Other legal wrong

A printable version of this topic map is available from **www.pearsoned.co.uk/lawexpress**

■ Introduction

Sacred secrets

That is how the Hippocratic oath describes the information given by patients to doctors. The oath requires doctors not to reveal these secrets. The law likewise requires doctors generally to keep confidential information, well, confidential. Of course, the issue is not as straightforward as that. The law accepts that there are circumstances in which confidentiality can, indeed sometimes should, be breached. Although quite what these are is unclear. Further, there are the difficulties over what information is protected by confidentiality. Is everything one says to a doctor covered, or only medical matters?

ASSESSMENT ADVICE

Essay questions

There are three major topics which are the most likely to be the subject of an essay question in the exam. The first is the source of the obligation of confidentiality. While there is widespread agreement that medical secrets should be kept confidential, the exact legal basis for this is unclear. The second is the circumstances in which it is permissible to breach confidentiality. You will need to be able to discuss the circumstances in which the law may permit such breaches, but also to consider whether these are justifiable. The third is the special issues surrounding genetic information. Here you will need to discuss to whom the genetic information belongs and whether there is a right not to know.

Problem questions

These are likely to centre on a scenario where there is doubt over whether a piece of information is protected by medical confidentiality. You are also likely to have to discuss whether the disclosure of such information is justified in legal terms. As always, make sure that you discuss what the law is, rather than what you think the law should be. Notice that the law is rather unclear on when disclosure of confidential information is justified. There may be, therefore, no clearly right or wrong answer, and rather the examiner is wanting you to set out the arguments that could be put on either side, based on what the case law has told us.

■ Sample question

Could you answer this question? Below is a typical essay question that could arise on this topic. Guidelines on answering the question are included at the end of this chapter, whilst a sample problem question and guidance on tackling it can be found on the companion website.

ESSAY QUESTION

Does the law ever permit a healthcare professional to disclose confidential medical information? Should it ever be permissible to disclose such information?

■ The basis in law for confidentiality

Surprisingly, it is not easy to locate the legal basis for protecting confidential information. Revealing confidential information could amount to any of the following legal wrongs.

- a breach of contract
- negligence and so giving rise to a remedy in the law of tort
- an equitable wrong
- a criminal offence
- a breach of someone's human rights
- a breach of a statutory obligation
- a breach of a professional code of practice.

✎ EXAM TIP

In an exam you will want to show a knowledge of all of these potential bases of claim, but focus on those you think most appropriate. Note, for example, that NHS patients do not have a contract with their doctors and so they could not rely on a breach of contract claim. From an ethical point of view, there are two main principles behind the protection of medical information. The first is that it protects the patients' right to privacy. Second, it has the benefit of meaning that patients can trust their doctors and tell them anything. This should ensure that the best diagnosis can be given.

Of these, the basis which appears to be used the most often, and which, therefore, is the most important, is the equitable wrong. The elements of this are set out in the table below.

Elements of equitable breach of confidence	Authority
The information must be personal, private or intimate	*Campbell* v. *Mirror Group Newspapers* (2004)
The information must be imparted in circumstances which impose an obligation of confidence	*Venables* v. *Mirror Group Newspapers* (2001)
An unauthorised person must see the information	*A-G* v. *Guardian Newspapers* (1990)

The elements of the equitable wrong were considered in the following case.

KEY CASE

Campbell v. *Mirror Group Newspapers* [2004] UKHL 22

Concerning: the legal basis for protecting confidential information

Facts

Naomi Campbell (the supermodel) was photographed leaving a meeting of Narcotics Anonymous. The photograph was published by the *Daily Mirror*. Ms Campbell sued for breach of confidence.

Legal principle

Their Lordships held that Campbell's attendance at Narcotics Anonymous meetings was confidential. The protection of confidential information concerned 'the right to control the dissemination of information about one's private life and the right to the esteem and respect of other people' (Lord Hoffmann). Lord Hoffmann and Baroness Hale said that if a person would have a reasonable expectation that information would be kept confidential, it was protected by the law. Applying this to the facts of the case, the majority of their Lordships held that attendance for treatment of a drug addiction would be confidential. However, Naomi Campbell had spoken in public about her problems with drugs and so the mere fact she was receiving treatment was not protected. But she had not revealed the details about her treatment and so these were protected. Their Lordships explained that it was necessary to weigh up the right to protection of confidential information with the right of freedom of expression. Both of these rights were protected by the European Convention on Human Rights. The majority found in this case that the balance fell in favour of protecting the right of confidentiality, rather than freedom of expression. Notably the damages awarded were on the low side (£2,500). Baroness Hale's comment suggested that their Lordships had no great sympathy for either side: 'Put crudely, it is a prima donna celebrity against a celebrity-exploiting tabloid newspaper.'

A good answer will show awareness of the potential impact of the Human Rights Act. Note that Article 8 of the ECHR protects confidential information. However, remember that you cannot sue simply for a breach of an ECHR article. What, however, a court may do in deciding how to develop the law on equitable breach of confidence is to consider what rights the parties have under the ECHR (see *Campbell* v. *MGN*, where they did this). Most significantly, under Article 10 there is the important right to free speech. The courts will weigh up the public importance in the issue at hand, and the harm to the individual by publication when deciding whether the right to free speech should carry more weight than the right to protection of confidential information.

The professional disciplinary bodies (e.g. the British Medical Association (BMA), the Nursing and Midwifery Council) have produced guidelines on confidentiality. In practice, many healthcare professionals follow the guidance of their professional body, and trust that in doing so they are in compliance with the law. You therefore need to be aware of the guidance that has been issued (see Herring (2012, chapter 3) for a summary of these).

■ When is disclosure of confidential information permitted?

Once it is established that the information is protected as confidential information, the next issue to consider is whether the disclosure is justified.

Consent

Fairly obviously, if the patient has consented to the disclosure, there is no breach of confidentiality. Hence, if a doctor passes on a patient's medical records to a consultant, at the patient's request, there is no breach.

Anonymous

In a controversial decision it has been held that the release of medical information in an anonymous form (e.g. with the patient's name deleted) does not breach confidentiality.

KEY CASE

R v. Department of Health ex p. Source Informatics **[2001] QB 424**

Concerning: whether anonymous information is confidential

Facts

Source Informatics Ltd was a company which sold information to drugs companies. It arranged for GPs and pharmacists to pass information to it. The information did not include the name of the patient, only the doctor's name and the drug prescribed. The Department of Health said that this breached confidentiality. Source Informatics sought a ruling that the Department of Health's guidance was incorrect.

Legal principle

The guidance was improper. As the patients' names were removed and there was no identifying information, the patients' privacy was not infringed. The doctors and pharmacists who had passed on the information could not be said to be breaching their duty of good faith.

✓ Make your answer stand out

The *Source Informatics* decision is controversial. A good answer will be aware of the controversy. Do you think it correct that if your medical information is rendered anonymous you really have no objection to it being distributed? What if the information was used for medical research to which you had moral objections? If it is anonymous, is it really still 'your' information? See Case (2003) for further discussion. In *Department of Health* v. *Information Commissioner* (2011) the Government was required to release anonymous data about abortions. Does that worry you?

The proper working of the hospital

In *R* v. *Department of Health ex p. Source Informatics Ltd* (2001) Simon Brown LJ held that information passed within the NHS for legitimate purposes was justifiable. This might include information passed between NHS professionals and used for the purposes of treatment, audit or research (Health and Social Care Act 2001, s. 60).

A threat of serious harm to others

As the following case shows, one justification for revealing confidential information is that to do so would avoid a threat of serious harm to others. This, for example, would cover a case where a man revealed to his doctor that he was abusing his child. In such a case, a doctor would be entitled to disclose that information to the relevant authorities.

KEY CASE

W v. *Edgell* [1990] 1 All ER 835

Concerning: when confidentiality can be breached

Facts

W had been detained in a secure mental hospital after a conviction for manslaughter of five people. A mental health review tribunal was considering whether W was safe to be released, and a report was commissioned from Dr Edgell. His report suggested that W was extremely dangerous. He wanted to show the report to the director of the hospital caring for W because he thought that the hospital did not realise how dangerous W was. W sought an order to prevent the disclosure of the report.

Legal principle

The Court of Appeal held that it was justifiable to disclose the report to the Home Office and the director of the hospital. The court held that the public interest justified the disclosure. There was real risk of significant harm to others.

✎ EXAM TIP

A point to emphasise in an exam answer is that simply because it may be justified to make a disclosure does not mean you can disclose the information to anyone. In *W* v. *Edgell* it was found to be permissible for the doctor to disclose the report to the director of the hospital or the Home Office. It would not have been permissible to disclose the information to a newspaper.

 Make your answer stand out

A good issue to consider in an essay on confidentiality is a case where it is discovered that a patient is HIV positive. The patient is in a long-term relationship but does not want to tell their partner. Of course, a doctor should encourage the patient to disclose their status, but what if the patient refuses? Could this be a case where breach of confidentiality is justified in the name of protecting others from serious harm? Or would doing that undermine the trust that potentially HIV patients have in their doctors?

Assisting police investigations

Rather oddly, there is only a very limited obligation on a doctor to disclose to the police that a patient has confessed to having committed a crime. They are required to disclose information (if requested to by police) if a driver is alleged to have committed a traffic offence (Road Traffic Act 1988, s. 172). The BMA encourages doctors to disclose information if the offence is grave; the detection of the crime will be seriously delayed or prejudiced without the disclosure; and if the disclosure would only be used for the detection and prosecution of the alleged offender.

Press freedom

There may be cases where the disclosure of confidential information by a newspaper is justified in the name of generating public debate and press freedom. In *H (A Healthcare Worker)* v. *Associated Newspapers* (2002) the Court of Appeal held that a newspaper could inform the public that a healthcare professional had tested positive for HIV and disclose his specialism. However, his name and employer could not be revealed.

■ Genetic information

> **KEY DEFINITION: Genetic information**
>
> This is medical information about your genes, including your DNA. This can reveal whether you have a genetically related illness or whether you are a carrier of one.

As a basic rule, **genetic information** is entitled to the same kind of protection as any other medical information. The difficulty is that genetic information about A may reveal genetic information about B. For example, informing a patient that they have a certain genetic condition may mean the patient will realise that either their mother or father has that condition. The courts are yet to discuss how the traditional approach to medical confidentiality applies in such a context (see Skene (2001)). Another troublesome issue is whether employers or insurers can require individuals to undertake genetic tests to see if they are likely to develop illnesses in the future. While such tests would be very useful to employers and insurers, they are likely to lead to a situation where people with 'bad' genetic make-ups are unable to find jobs or obtain insurance.

> ✓ Make your answer stand out
>
> Be familiar with the debates over the right *not* to know. Imagine that a doctor has discovered that patient A has a serious terminal illness. Patient A has a brother (B) and it is likely that B also has the condition. Should B be told by the doctor? Might B rather not know of the risk that they have the condition, especially if there is no available treatment? On the other hand, B might well want to know so they can plan the last few years (if they have the condition) of their life. The problem is that the doctor cannot find out whether B is the kind of person who will want to know the medical truth, or would rather not. See Laurie (2002) and Andorno (2004) for a further discussion of this.

A right to access information

There is a right to access medical information held by a doctor. The most important rights can be found under the Data Protection Act 1998 and Access to Medical Reports Act 1998. Even there, disclosure can be refused if it would cause serious harm to the physical or mental health of the patient or someone else.

Putting it all together

Answer guidelines

See the essay question at the start of the chapter.

Approaching the question

This essay question is in two parts. The first focuses on the circumstances in which it is permissible to breach medical confidence. The second half of the essay should look at whether a breach is ever justified. This provides you with a neat way of structuring the essay.

Important points to include

In the first half, looking at when it is permissible to breach medical confidence will focus on the current law. The examiner does not want you to spend much time describing what information is protected by medical confidence, although an introductory paragraph summarising that would be useful. The focus of the first half should be going through the different circumstances in which a breach is justified (e.g. W v. Edgell). Don't forget the relevance of the Human Rights Act (Campbell v. MGN).

The second half of the essay should look at whether a breach is ever justified. Note that, although you might conclude that in a particular circumstance greater good will come from a breach than preservation, you will need to consider the wider ramifications that might flow if medical secrets are not strictly protected. In other words, although breach in this particular case may appear justified if the effect of such a breach is that people no longer trust their doctors, this may have harmful effects overall. It would be good to consider the special issues that are raised by genetic information.

✓ Make your answer stand out

A very good answer will look at why the law thinks it is important to protect
confidence. Only when you have done that can you consider when confidences
should be breached. Notice that some arguments about protection of confidence
are based on the public good and some are based on fundamental moral
principles.

READ TO IMPRESS

Andorno, R. (2004) 'The Right Not to Know: an autonomy based approach', 30 *Journal of Medical Ethics* 435.

Case, P. (2003) 'Confidence Matters: the rise and fall of informational autonomy in medical law', 11 *Medical Law Review* 208.

Herring, J. (2012) *Medical Law and Ethics.* Oxford: Oxford University Press.

Kottow, M. (1986) 'Medical Confidentiality: an absolute and intransigent obligation', 12 *Journal of Medical Ethics* 117.

Laurie, G. (2002) *Genetic Privacy.* Cambridge: Cambridge University Press.

Mikalowski, S. (2004) *Medical Confidentiality and Crime.* Oxford: Oxford University Press.

Skene, L. (2001) 'Genetic Secrets and the Family', 6 *Medical Law Review* 1.

Taylor, M. (2011) 'Health Research, Data Protection, and the Public Interest in Notification', 19 *Medical Law Review* 267.

www.pearsoned.co.uk/lawexpress

Go online to access more revision support including quizzes to test your
knowledge, sample questions with answer guidelines, podcasts you can
download, and more!

Medical negligence

5

Revision checklist

Essential points you should know:

☐ When a healthcare professional owes a patient a duty of care

☐ How the court decides whether there has been a breach of a duty of care

☐ How damages are assessed

☐ Alternatives to the current law on medical errors

■ Topic map

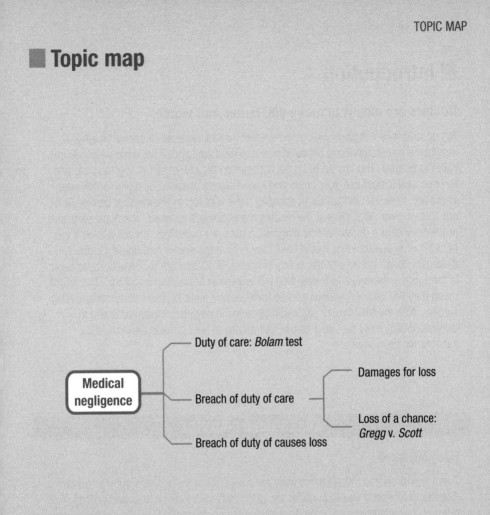

- Medical negligence
  - Duty of care: *Bolam* test
  - Breach of duty of care
    - Damages for loss
    - Loss of a chance: *Gregg* v. *Scott*
  - Breach of duty of causes loss

�e Introduction

Doctors are meant to make you better, not worse.

But occasionally things go wrong and a court may be required to decide whether a healthcare professional has behaved in a negligent way and, if so, what damages are liable to be paid. The law on this area is based on the law of tort. If you have studied tort law, you should use your notes and knowledge to answer questions in this area. There are, however, difficulties in applying the law of tort in the medical context. It is not always clear what caused the injuries the victim has suffered. There are particular problems where a doctor fails to diagnose a patient's condition. In such a case it can be difficult to predict what would have happened if the doctor had made a correct diagnosis. There are also public policy concerns. If doctors are too readily found liable in negligence, there is a fear that they will engage in 'defensive medicine'. This might mean they will be overcautious and do unnecessary tests or refuse to undertake risky surgery. Also the NHS has to pay out large sums in negligence payments and to lawyers. Would it not be better to use this money to help provide better medical services for everyone?

ASSESSMENT ADVICE

Essay questions

There is widespread unhappiness with the law in this area, and so a popular essay question will require you to consider the difficulties with the law here and possible reforms. You might also be asked to consider the controversial '*Bolam* test' for medical negligence (see Chapter 5). The essay is likely to ask you to analyse the meaning of the test as well as debate whether or not it is appropriate. Another issue which could arise in this area is 'loss of a chance'. This topic is one where a detailed knowledge of the case law is essential. You should also consider some of the alternatives to the system based on negligence such as the redress schemes created under the NHS Redress Act 2006 and the possibility of adopting a 'no fault' system.

Problem questions

These are likely to require you to consider a number of aspects of the law of negligence. You will need to be able to apply the *Bolam* test. As we shall see, there is much debate over how the *Bolam* test should be applied and whether recent cases have diluted it or not. You should pay particular attention to this debate and the cases that can be used to support either a stricter or weaker version of the *Bolam* test. You may also be required to consider how the 'loss of a chance' case law applies in a particular scenario. The recent case of *Chester* v. *Afshar* is worth knowing very well. The examiners may set a problem question which is similar, but not identical, to the facts of that case. You will need to know why the House of Lords decided that case the way it did. There may also be issues relating to the level of damages that have to be paid, although you will not be required to provide an exact figure as to how much the court will award.

■ Sample question

Could you answer this question? Below is a typical problem question that could arise on this topic. Guidelines on answering the question are included at the end of this chapter, whilst a sample essay question and guidance on tackling it can be found on the companion website.

PROBLEM QUESTION

Penelope is experiencing pain in her back. She is referred to a consultant, Dr House. Dr House recommends a novel form of surgery for her back pain. He fails to tell her that there is a small risk of permanent paralysis from the surgery. While performing the surgery, he sneezes and this causes an involuntary movement which causes Penelope a serious internal injury. The operation is unsuccessful and leaves her permanently paralysed. The internal injury causes her severe pain, for which there is no effective treatment. At the trial, Penelope accepts that she was in such pain that even if Dr House had informed her of the risk of paralysis, she would probably have agreed to go ahead with the surgery, although she might have sought a second opinion. Expert evidence shows that there is only a handful of experts in this field who approve of the novel form of surgery carried out by Dr House. Most think it too risky. Expert evidence also shows that any competent surgeon would be aware of the risks of sneezing and would have taken steps to ensure that it would not affect the patient. However, it was accepted that there were many reported cases of injuries caused by sneezing.

Discuss whether Penelope can successfully sue Dr House for negligence.

■ The basic principles of the law of negligence

In order successfully to bring a claim of negligence, it is necessary to show three things:

- the professional who is being sued owed the claimant a duty of care
- the professional breached the duty of care
- the breach of the duty of care caused the claimant loss.

The duty of care

KEY DEFINITION: Duty of care

In the law of tort, a person owes a duty of care to all those whom that person may foreseeably harm. Occasionally, the courts hold that there are good public-policy reasons for not finding a duty of care.

There is normally little difficulty in finding that a doctor owes a patient a **duty of care**. This is because the basic rule is that a person owes a duty of care to anyone they may foreseeably injure. Of course, it is foreseeable that there is a risk of injury whenever a medical professional provides treatment to a patient. The issue can arise where a doctor comes across an injured person while going about their everyday business and offers no treatment. Normally, a person is not liable in tort for failing to help someone, unless there is a special relationship between them. It appears that if a doctor comes across a patient who is on their books, the doctor must offer assistance, but if they have no connection to the injured person, the doctor is free to walk on by. That was suggested in *F* v. *West Berkshire Health Authority* (1989). Another issue is whether a doctor owes a duty of care to the relatives or friends of a patient (see *Goodwill* v. *BPAS* (1996) where a doctor was held to owe a duty of care to his patient, but not to those the patient would go on to have sexual relations with).

Breach of the duty of care

Normally in the law of tort, a person breaches a duty of care if they behave in a way in which a reasonable person in their shoes would not act. However, the test in relation to medical negligence (where the claim is against a healthcare professional) is slightly different. It is set out in the following case.

KEY CASE

Bolam v. *Friern Hospital Management Committee* **[1957] 2 All ER 118**
Concerning: when a doctor is liable in negligence

Facts

John Bolam suffered a depressive illness. He was advised by a consultant to have electroconvulsive therapy. He was not told of the risk of bone fracture nor was he given relaxant drugs. He suffered several injuries. He sued the consultant in negligence.

Legal principle

McNair J held that the correct test to determine whether the consultant had behaved negligently was to ask whether he was acting 'in accordance with a practice of competent and respected medical opinion'. He went on to say, 'A doctor is not guilty of negligence if he has acted in accordance with a practice accepted as proper by a responsible body of medical men skilled in that particular art.' Here the consultant had and so he was not liable in negligence.

✎ EXAM TIP

It is important to appreciate the significance of the *Bolam* test. It means that, even though a majority of doctors would not have acted as the defendant did, if the defendant can show that a group of respected doctors would have acted in the same way, they can have a defence. However, note the requirement that it is a respected body of opinion. It would not be enough to point to a couple of dodgy websites which recommend the treatment! Notice also that a doctor is judged on what the current thinking of experts was at the time when they acted, not what the current state of knowledge is (*Roe* v. *Minister of Health* (1954)). So, if the doctor's action was acceptable at the time they acted, the doctor would not be negligent, even if at the date of trial there was agreement that the action was inappropriate.

As a result of the *Bolam* test, if a doctor can show that a respected body of medical opinion would support their approach, they will have a defence (*Ecclestone* v. *Medway NHS Trust* (2013)).

Part of the thinking behind this is that if doctors disagreed among themselves over what treatment was best, it would not be right for a judge to decide between two competing schools of medical opinion. The judge is not in a position to determine which school of thought was better. Note also that a doctor is only expected to show the degree of skill expected of someone of their specialism or profession. A GP is not expected to show the same skill as a consultant specialist. Also a doctor can only be judged on the facts they could have known about at the time. So, the fact a patient later developed an illness does not mean the doctor should have spotted it at the time if there was no way they could have known about it (*Ministry of Justice* v. *Carter* (2010)). Similarly, if a patient fails to tell a doctor about one of his symptoms and as a result the doctor makes a misdiagnosis, the doctor will not be negligent (*Ingram* v. *Williams* (2010)).

> **!** Don't be tempted to . . .
>
> When discussing when a judge can declare a body of opinion to be not respectable
> it is important to take care in discussing the law. In *Bolitho* v. *City and Hackney Health
> Authority* (1998) Lord Browne-Wilkinson appeared to suggest that if a judge decided
> that a particular view had no logical basis, it could be declared not logical. Some
> commentators (see Teff (1998)) thought this was a major shift in approach as it
> required the judge to subject the views of experts to some degree of scrutiny. Indeed,
> in *Marriott* v. *West Midlands Health Authority* (1999) although there was evidence that
> some doctors would approve of the way the doctor acted in not ordering further tests,
> their views were branded irresponsible. However, other cases have suggested it would
> be very rare for a judge to brand a school of medical opinion as irresponsible (see e.g.
> *M* v. *Blackpool Victoria Hospital NHS Trust* (2003)).

Causation

It must be shown that the negligence caused the patient's loss. So, if it could be shown, that
despite the negligence of the doctor no loss resulted from it, there will be no liability to pay
damages. This means that a doctor may be negligent in not ordering further tests, but if those
tests would not have revealed the illness of the patient, no damages will be payable. Similarly,
if the doctor was negligent in failing to correctly diagnose the patient, there is no liability if,
even if the correct diagnosis had been made, nothing could have been done to help the patient
(*Wright* v. *Cambridge Medical Group* (2011)). Where it is unclear whether the cause of the
patient's condition was due to negligence or some other cause, no claim in negligence can
be brought (*Wilsher* v. *Essex Area Health Authority* (1987)). It must be shown that it is more
likely than not that the negligence caused the loss. However, the courts may be willing to
presume causation, using the principle *res ipsa loquitur*. In *Thomas* v. *Curley* (2013) an
injury had occurred during an operation. It was not possible to prove how it had happened,
but the court held that as the doctor had not been able to provide a plausible alternative
explanation, it was presumed to have occurred as a result of the negligence of the doctor.

> **KEY DEFINITION:** *Res ipsa loquitur*
>
> Literally translated, 'the act speaks for itself'. It is a doctrine used in the law of
> negligence where there is no reasonable explanation for an injury apart from the fact
> the defendant must have caused the injury negligently.

Loss of a chance cases

The most difficult cases are those where, as a result of the negligence of a healthcare
professional, a patient has lost a chance of being offered an effective treatment. The
following are the two key legal cases.

KEY CASE

Hotson v. *East Berkshire Area Health Authority* **[1987] AC 750**

Concerning: when a claim can be brought for a 'loss of a chance'

Facts

A boy, 13, fell out of a tree. His hip was injured and he was taken to hospital. The nature and severity of his injury was not appreciated and he did not receive proper treatment. He developed a serious disability of the hip joint. The evidence suggested that if the proper treatment had been given, there would have been a 25 per cent chance that he would recover. He sued, claiming that the failure to provide proper treatment had deprived him of a 25 per cent chance of an effective recovery.

Legal principle

The House of Lords rejected the approach of the trial judge who had given the boy 25 per cent of the damages he would have got if it had been shown that the medical team's negligence had caused the injury. As a general rule, their Lordships held that damages could only be awarded if it could be shown that if properly treated there would have been a greater than 50 per cent chance of recovery. So here he could not be awarded any damages.

KEY CASE

Gregg v. *Scott* **[2005] UKHL 2**

Concerning: when a patient can recover damages for a 'loss of a chance'

Facts

Mr Gregg consulted Dr Scott about a lump under his arm. Scott negligently diagnosed the lump as benign. It was later discovered that Gregg suffered from cancer of the lymph gland and there was a poor prognosis. The judge found that if properly diagnosed at the time, Gregg would have had a 42 per cent chance of surviving for 10 years or more, but now it was 25 per cent.

Legal principle

Mr Gregg lost his case. It had not been shown that on the balance of probabilities if he had been properly diagnosed he would have been cured. Even if properly diagnosed, the most likely scenario was that he would be in the same position that he was now. One powerful argument which influenced their Lordships was that if the claim were allowed, the impact on the NHS could be enormous.

These cases emphasise that only if it can be shown that if the defendant had not acted negligently it would be more likely than not that they would not have suffered the loss (i.e. there was at least a 50 per cent chance of being given successful treatment).

✓ **Make your answer stand out**

You should note that this is a controversial approach for the courts to take. Read both the dissenting as well as the majority judgments in *Gregg*. Note two objections, in particular, to the current law. First, a patient who would have a 45 per cent chance of surviving cancer but now, as a result of negligence, has only a 5 per cent chance will feel that they have suffered a genuine loss. Should the law not recognise this? Second, is it right that a doctor can behave negligently, but then escape liability by saying that the patient would probably be just as badly off if they had acted properly? Notice also the emphasis in *Gregg* v. *Scott* placed on the possible financial costs to the NHS if a patient could claim for a 'loss of a chance'. Is it fair that such an argument should play a role in developing the case law? Could not the same point be made for any sort of claim against the NHS?

Failure to warn of a risk

The leading case on this is the following:

KEY CASE

Chester v. *Afshar* [2004] UKHL 41

Concerning: when a doctor was liable for failing to warn of a risk

Facts

Ms Chester suffered back pain. Her consultant, Mr Afshar, recommended surgery but failed to warn her of the one to two per cent chance of severe nerve damage. The operation was performed properly but nerve damage resulted and she was partially paralysed. The court found that if Ms Chester had been warned of the operation, she would have eventually agreed to the operation, but at a later time, having sought further advice.

Legal principle

Ms Chester was entitled to damages. Had she been warned of the risk, she would not have consented to have the operation at the time she did. It was true that she would have consented to the operation later and it would have carried the same risks as the operation she had. Nevertheless, there was a sufficient causal link between the negligence of Dr Afshar and the injuries suffered by Ms Chester. Their Lordships were influenced by the importance they attached to the requirements that doctors should warn patients of the risks that medical procedures carried. They should not be able to breach those duties and then escape liability in tort.

It is important to realise the limits of this case. Notice that it was crucial that the claimant was able to demonstrate that if she had been informed of the risks, she would have had the operation at a different time because she would have sought other advice. It seems if the evidence had shown that she would have had the operation at the same time, she would have lost the case.

✓ **Make your answer stand out**

When revising, have a good think about the decision in *Chester* v. *Afshar*. Do you think the decision in *Chester* v. *Afshar* was motivated as much by a wish to punish a doctor who behaved negligently as it was to compensate the complainant for her loss? What, in fact, was her loss here? She accepts that, but for the negligence, she would have had the operation anyway, and the operation would have been as risky as the one she had. Was her real loss a lack of proper information? Notice the emphasis placed on patients' rights to be informed of risks in the majority's judgments. Some commentators suggest that a similar emphasis on patients' rights was not found in *Gregg* v. *Scott*. Do not patients also have a right to be diagnosed with reasonable skill?

Harm to secondary victims

The law of tort is generally reluctant to award damages to a person who is psychologically harmed by witnessing harm suffered by others. Therefore, where a patient is harmed by the negligence of a doctor, it is unlikely that the relatives of a patient will be able to sue for damages for the psychological distress they suffer at seeing the patient suffer. However, there is no complete bar on such a claim if a relative is actually in the room when the patient is negligently injured. Relatives may also be able to claim if their distress was directly caused by the negligence of a healthcare professional. This might be where they are told in a particularly callous way that their relative has died.

■ Damages

The damages available following a successful medical negligence claim follow the same principles as general tort law. They can include expenses incurred as a result of the injuries, loss of earnings due to the injury, and compensation for pain and suffering.

■ The NHS Redress Act 2006

There has been increasing dissatisfaction with the way that the current law on medical negligence works. Some believe litigation encourages the NHS and its staff to become antagonistic towards patients who have been injured. It might even discourage doctors from being honest when something has gone wrong, for fear that they will be sued. Certainly, the legal costs to the NHS and patients are huge. Often the legal costs exceed the costs of any damages the courts award. Some research has suggested that what patients who have been harmed by bad medical practice really want is an apology and a reassurance that a similar thing will not happen to other people, but there is no ready means of doing that apart from suing. The NHS Redress Act 2006 allows the Secretary of State to set up a more informal process by which a person with a complaint against the NHS can use a redress scheme which will not involve going to court. Where a complaint is made, the patient may receive an apology, an explanation, a report of what will happen to ensure there will not be a repetition and/or compensation.

✎ EXAM TIP

You may be asked in the exam to consider the problems with the current law. In doing so, you should consider the effectiveness of schemes created under the NHS Redress Act 2006. Some commentators have suggested that if a patient is harmed as a result of medical treatment, they should receive compensation whether or not there was fault on the part of doctors. Schemes based on this approach are used in some countries, such as New Zealand. Their supporters claim that this will mean there will be less stigma attaching to doctors found to have caused harm to a patient, and that might mean that they will be more open about what has happened. It is also said that it avoids the difficulty the law faces in finding whether or not a doctor has been negligent. Opponents of such 'no fault' schemes argue that, if a doctor has behaved negligently, it is in the public interest that this be made known. There is also a major concern that a no fault scheme would cost the NHS huge sums of money.

■ The licensing of medicines

There are special rules that deal with the development and manufacture of medicines. These are governed by the Medicines Act 1968. It is likely in future that there will be European guidelines controlling this area.

■ Regulation by professional or NHS bodies

As well as regulation by the courts, there are professional and NHS bodies which regulate medical professionals. These include organisations such as the General Medical Council and National Patient Safety. These bodies can bar professionals from acting by striking them off the relevant professional register. They can also require professionals to undergo further training or bar them from acting in a particular area.

■ Putting it all together

Answer guidelines

See the problem question at the start of the chapter.

Approaching the question

In dealing with problem questions concerning medical negligence, it is helpful to keep separate three key issues. First, whether the doctor owed a duty of care. Second, whether there was a breach of that duty. Third, whether the breach of the duty caused a loss. Keep these three issues separate in your answer.

Important points to include

There is no problem here in establishing that Dr House owes Penelope a duty of care. The question is whether he breaches the duty. Note that there are three claims here. The first is that he was negligent in the way he did the operation. The *Bolam* test would need to be applied: is there a respectable body of opinion which holds it appropriate to do surgery if you are prone to sneezing?

The second claim is whether it was appropriate to do this kind of surgery at all, given that many doctors believe it too risky. Again, the *Bolam* test would need to be considered. A good answer would examine whether the subsequent case law has diluted the *Bolam* test at all.

The third (and this is harder) is the failure to warn of the risks. Here *Chester* v. *Afshar* will need to be considered. In *Chester* much weight was attached to the fact that if properly warned of the risks, the patient would not have agreed to have the operation at the time she had it.

If there is a breach, you will need to consider how the court will award damages. Notice that the damages in *Chester* v. *Afshar* appear to match the amount to cover the injury suffered.

✓ **Make your answer stand out**

Make good use of the case law. In particular consider whether the decision in *Bolitho* has changed the general approach taken in *Bolam*. A good answer will also contain a careful analysis of the decision in *Chester*. Remember in that case it was essential to the success of the case that the claimant would have had the operation at a different time.

READ TO IMPRESS

Brazier, M. and Miola, J. (2000) 'Bye-Bye Bolam: a medical litigation revolution', 8 *Medical Law Review* 85.

Davies, M. (2006) *Medical Self-Regulation*. Aldershot: Ashgate.

Douglas, T. (2009) 'Medical Compensation: beyond "no fault"', 17 *Medical Law Review* 30.

Harris, J. (1997) 'The Injustice of Compensation for Victims of Medical Accidents', 314 *British Medical Journal* 1821.

Maclean, A. (2012) 'From Sidaway to Pearce', 20 *Medical Law Review* 108.

Merry, A. and McCall Smith, R. A. (2001) *Errors, Medicine and the Law*. Cambridge: Cambridge University Press.

Mulheron, R. (2010) 'Trumping Bolam: a critical legal analysis of Bolitho's "gloss"', 69 *Cambridge Law Journal* 609.

Quick, O. (2010) 'Medicine, Mistakes and Manslaughter: a criminal combination', 69 *Cambridge Law Journal* 186.

Teff, H. (1998) 'The Standard of Care in Medical Negligence – Moving on from *Bolam*?', 18 *Oxford Journal of Legal Studies* 473.

Lord Woolf (2000) 'Are the Courts Excessively Deferential to the Medical Profession?', 9 *Medical Law Review* 1.

www.pearsoned.co.uk/lawexpress

Go online to access more revision support including quizzes to test your knowledge, sample questions with answer guidelines, podcasts you can download, and more!

Contraception, abortion and pregnancy

6

Revision checklist

Essential points you should know:

- [ ] The difference between contraception and abortion
- [ ] The circumstances in which an abortion is legal
- [ ] The circumstances in which a woman can be forced to have a Caesarean section without her consent

■ Topic map

The difference between abortion and contraception

Grounds for abortion
- Risk of injury to woman
- Risk of grave permanent injury to woman
- Risk to the life of woman
- Risk of physical or mental abnormalities to fetus

Regulation of pregnancy
- Right to refuse treatment: *St George's NHS Trust* v. *S*
- Best interests test used if competent: Mental Capacity Act

■ Introduction

When does life begin?

This is a question which has been troubling lawyers, philosophers and politicians for centuries. Yet, it is central to the debates over abortion and pregnancy. It is easy for the debates over these issues to become polarised between those who are 'pro-life' and those who are 'pro-choice'. Pro-lifers claim that human life begins at conception or shortly thereafter. The law should therefore protect the life of the unborn child with as much rigour as it protects other human life. Pro-choicers emphasise that it should be a woman's right to choose what should happen to her body and her fetus. Most legal systems are a compromise between these views: not treating the fetus with the same rights as an adult, but neither allowing a woman to do whatever she wants with the fetus.

ASSESSMENT ADVICE

Essay questions

These will require you to demonstrate a good knowledge of the law as well as an awareness of the ethical debates surrounding the subjects. Be careful not to get carried away when writing your essay. You need to show a sensitivity to the complex issues that surround this subject. Even if you have strong views, you need to discuss respectfully the views of others and explain carefully why you disagree. Do not assume that the extreme 'pro-choice' or 'pro-life' views are the only ones available; there is a range of compromise positions as well which you should consider.

Problem questions

The two most likely areas to arise as problem questions would be abortion or enforced Caesarean section cases. In relation to abortion, you will need to have a detailed knowledge of the Abortion Act 1967 and the criminal offences which will be committed if that Act is not complied with. In relation to cases surrounding enforced Caesarean sections, you will need to separate out two key questions. First, does the woman have capacity to consent to the operation? Second, if she lacks capacity, would the operation be in her best interests? Alternatively, if she has capacity, how does the law treat a competent refusal in this context? You will need to be able to discuss some of the leading cases on the topic.

■ Sample question

Could you answer this question? Below is a typical problem question that could arise on this topic. Guidelines on answering the question are included at the end of this chapter, whilst a sample essay question and guidance on tackling it can be found on the companion website.

■ Contraception

The law on **contraception** has had to move with the times. In the past the provision of contraception was heavily regulated. However, Munby J in *R (Smeaton)* v. *Secretary of State for Health* (2002) stated that contraception was 'no business of government, judges or the law'. In fact, section 5(1)(b) of the National Health Service Act 1977 requires the Secretary of State for Health to ensure that 'all reasonable requirements' for treatment and advice on contraceptive issues are met. The main legal issue concerning contraception is the dividing line between the provision of contraception and abortion. The provision of contraception is largely unregulated. While abortion is tightly controlled by the Abortion Act 1967, the distinction was explored in the following case.

KEY CASE

R (Smeaton) v. *Secretary of State for Health* [2002] 2 FCR 193

Concerning: the definition of contraception and miscarriage

Facts

The Society for the Protection of the Unborn Children (SPUC) challenged the legality of a statutory instrument which permitted the sale of the 'morning after pill' without prescription. The SPUC claimed that the use of the pill caused a miscarriage or abortion and, therefore, involved criminal offences under section 58 or 59 of the Offences Against the Person Act 1861. The use of the pill would, therefore, only be lawful if the requirements of the Abortion Act 1967 were satisfied. The government argued that the pill was contraception and so was not governed by the Act and could be given without prescription.

Legal principle

Munby J rejected the view that the word 'miscarriage' meant any procedure that caused the loss of a fertilised egg. A miscarriage only occurred where there had been an established pregnancy. Munby J also held that there would be harmful social effects if emergency contraception could only be given if the requirements of the Abortion Act 1967 were met. He, therefore, held that the 'morning after pill' could be sold without prescription and that using it would not amount to an offence.

KEY DEFINITION: Contraception

A procedure or device which prevents fertilisation of the egg or the implantation of the fertilised egg.

Abortion

To perform an abortion without legal authority is a criminal offence. The two main offences which could be committed are contained in the following statutes.

KEY STATUTE

Offences Against the Person Act 1861, section 58

Every woman, being with child, who, with intent to procure her own miscarriage, shall unlawfully administer to herself any poison or other noxious thing, or shall unlawfully use any instrument or other means whatsoever with the like intent and whosoever, with intent to procure the miscarriage of any woman, whether she be or not with child, shall unlawfully administer to her or cause or be taken by her any poison or other noxious thing, or shall unlawfully use any instrument or other means whatsoever with the like intent, shall be guilty of an offence . . .

KEY STATUTE

Infant Life Preservation Act 1929, section 1

. . . any person who, with intent to destroy the life of a child capable of being born alive, by any wilful act causes a child to die before it has an existence independent of its mother, shall be guilty of an offence . . . Provided that no person shall be found guilty of an offence under this section unless it is proved that the act which caused the death of the child was not done in good faith for the purpose only of preserving the life of the mother.

! Don't be tempted to . . .

Sometimes students make the mistake of thinking English law overtly recognises there is a right to an abortion. But, notice that the starting point for the law is that an abortion is a criminal offence. The Abortion Act 1967 sets out the circumstances in which doctors have a defence to what would otherwise be a crime. It is, therefore, somewhat misleading to say that the Abortion Act 1967 protects the right to have an abortion (see Fox (1998)). Indeed (as we shall see), in the legislation it is the view of the doctors, rather than the choice of the woman, which is seen as key to the legality. It might be argued that a right to an abortion can be found through the Human Rights Act 1998.

EXAM TIP

In the unlikely event of a doctor being charged with performing an unlawful abortion, they would probably seek to argue that the procedure was permissible under the terms of the Abortion Act 1967. In an exam it is also worth referring to the defence of necessity at common law (*R* v. *Bourne* (1939)). It is not clear when this applies, but it certainly would be available where without the procedure the woman would die or suffer a serious harm.

The Abortion Act 1967

For an abortion to be lawful, the abortion must comply with the requirements of the 1967 Abortion Act. These are set out in the table below.

Requirement for an abortion to be lawful under the Act	Source
Abortions must be carried out under the authority of a registered medical practitioner	Abortion Act 1967, s. 1(1)
Abortions can only be carried out in an NHS Hospital or other approved place	Abortion Act 1967, s. 1(3)
All abortions must be notified to the Department of Health	Abortion Regulations 1991
Two medical practitioners must believe that at least one of the statutory grounds permitting abortion is made out	Abortion Act 1967, ss. 1(1)(a)–(d)

The statutory grounds for abortion are as follows.

Risk of injury to the health of the woman

KEY STATUTE

Abortion Act 1967, section 1(1)(a)

The pregnancy has not exceeded its twenty-fourth week and that the continuance of the pregnancy would involve risk, greater than if the pregnancy were terminated, of injury to the physical or mental health of the pregnant woman or any existing children of her family.

Notice that you can only rely on this ground if the pregnancy has not exceeded its twenty-fourth week. It needs to be shown first that there would be a risk to the physical or mental health of the woman or any of her existing children. And second, that this risk is greater if the pregnancy continued than if the pregnancy is terminated. It is unclear what an injury to mental health includes. Surely it would cover the risk of a woman suffering depression. But would it cover a risk of emotional upset? If so, this ground would be very broad indeed.

EXAM TIP

An examiner will be impressed if you are able to discuss the debates over when the twenty-fourth week is measured from. Is it from the date of conception, the date of implantation, the date of last period or first missed period? This is discussed in Herring (2012, chapter 8).

Grave permanent injury to the health of the woman

KEY STATUTE

Abortion Act 1967, section 1(1)(b)

The termination is necessary to prevent grave permanent injury to the physical or mental health of the pregnant woman.

This ground is harder to prove than section 1(1)(a). The harm involved to the woman needs to be grave, permanent, and an injury. Emotional upset would not, on its own, be sufficient to satisfy this ground. This ground can be used however far advanced the pregnancy is.

Risk to the life of the woman

KEY STATUTE

Abortion Act 1967, section 1(1)(c)

The continuance of the pregnancy would involve risk to the life of the pregnant woman, greater than if the pregnancy were terminated.

This is, perhaps, the least controversial ground for an abortion. Note that it only needs to be shown that there is a risk to the life of the woman. It does not need to be shown that this is necessarily a high risk.

Serious handicap of the child

KEY STATUTE

Abortion Act 1967, section 1(1)(d)

There is a substantial risk that if the child were born it would suffer from such physical or mental abnormalities as to be seriously handicapped.

This ground has no time limit and so can be used however far advanced the pregnancy is. There has been some debate over the words 'substantial' here and also over the word 'serious'. In 2005, a curate challenged the legality of an abortion of a fetus which had a cleft palate (see *Jepson* v. *Chief Constable of West Mercia* (2003)). The police in that case did not prosecute the doctor. This suggests that the definition of a serious handicap is not too difficult to satisfy.

✓ Make your answer stand out

There has been some dispute over the theoretical basis for the disability ground. A good answer will be able to discuss that. Is it suggesting that if a child is born seriously disabled, their life will be so appalling that it would have been better for the child not to be born? Or is the ground justified on the basis that the burden of caring for a seriously disabled child is so heavy that it should not be imposed on a reluctant parent. If the former, is this in effect a form of disability discrimination? Is the law saying that it would be better for disabled people not to be born? If it is the latter, might not the law say to a parent of a disabled person that if they are not willing to care for the child, then the state can arrange foster care or alternative arrangements? See Scott (2005) for further discussion of this issue.

✎ EXAM TIP

In an exam answer you should emphasise that the Abortion Act 1967 does not require that one of the four statutory grounds is, in fact, made out, but rather that two doctors were *of the opinion* that it is. In *Paton* v. *BPAS* (1979), George Baker P suggested that only if it were shown that the doctors were acting in clear bad faith would the statutory grounds not be made out. This also emphasises that it is the doctors' views on whether the grounds exist which matters, not the woman's. Note also that under the Abortion Act 1967, section 4, if a medical professional has a conscientious objection to abortion, they do not have to participate in an abortion. It has been claimed that in some parts of the country this has led to difficulties accessing abortion services.

Rights to abortion?

English law does not recognise a right to an abortion. A woman will need to persuade a doctor that one of the ground permitting abortion is established. The question of whether there is a right to abortion under the European Convention on Human Rights was considered in the following case.

KEY CASE

A, B and C v. *Ireland* [2010] ECHR 2032

Concerning: whether there is a right to an abortion

Facts

Three women from Ireland were not allowed abortions in Ireland, which has very strict laws permitting abortion only in very rare cases. Two of the women travelled to ▶

the UK so they could have an abortion. They claimed that their rights under the ECHR were infringed.

Legal principle

There was no general right to abortion under the ECHR. The issue was seen as morally controversial and so each signatory state could decide for itself what the correct approach of the law should be. One woman succeeded because it was insufficiently clear in her case whether the law permitted abortion. The court held that if a state's law did permit abortion, then it had to do so with sufficient clarity.

Attempts to stop abortions taking place

The courts have generally been very reluctant to make an order preventing an abortion or declaring that an abortion would be illegal. Courts have refused applications by fathers to prevent a mother having an abortion (*Paton* v. *BPAS* (1979)). Similarly unsuccessful have been attempts to bring proceedings 'in the name of the fetus' to prevent an abortion (*Paton* v. *BPAS* (1979)). Where a pregnant woman lacks capacity to decide whether or not to have an abortion, a decision will be made based on what is in her best interests (*Re SB* (2013)). Most controversially, it has been held in the following case that parents have no right to prevent their children from having abortions.

KEY CASE

R (on the application of Axon) v. *Secretary of State for Health (Family Planning Association intervening)* [2006] EWHC 37 (Admin)

Concerning: under-16-year-olds and the law on abortion

Facts

Mrs Sue Axon had two teenage daughters. She challenged official guidance issued by the Department of Health which allowed healthcare professionals to offer abortion services to under-16-year-olds without consultation with the child's parents. Mrs Axon claimed the guidance was unlawful and illegitimately interfered with her human rights as a parent.

Legal principle

Silber J held that if a young person was competent to consent, then abortion services could be offered and provided to her. Although the young person should be encouraged to inform her parents, there was no obligation for the parents to consent to such treatment or even be informed of it. Silber J held that the Human Rights Act 1998 did nothing to change the legal position on this.

In reaching the decision in *Axon*, the judge placed a lot of weight on the decision of the House of Lords in *Gillick* v. *West Norfolk and Wisbech Area Health Authority* (discussed in Chapter 3). Although from the discussion of the law on children and consent generally, in theory at least, even if a child did not want to have an abortion, a doctor could rely on the consent of her parent in order to give her one.

■ The legal status of the fetus

The legal status of the fetus is unclear. In *Attorney-General's Reference (No. 3 of 1994)* (1998) Lord Mustill described the fetus as a 'unique organism'. In *Vo* v. *France* (2005) it was held that a fetus had no right to life under the European Convention on Human Rights, but that it would not be contrary to the Convention for a country to enact legislation protecting the fetus. The following points can be made about the English law.

Legal points about a fetus	Authority
A fetus is not a person in the eyes of the law	*Attorney-General's Reference (No. 3 of 1994)* (1998)
A fetus is not simply part of the mother	*Attorney-General's Reference (No. 3 of 1994)* (1998)
It is not possible to bring proceedings 'in the name of the fetus'	*Paton* v. *BPAS* (1979)
A fetus cannot be made a ward of the court	*Re F (In Utero)* (1988)
A fetus has interests which are protected by the law	*St George's NHS Trust* v. *S* (1998)
A fetus is not directly protected by the European Convention on Human Rights	*Vo* v. *France* (2004)

✓ Make your answer stand out

The ethics of abortion are controversial and complex. An excellent answer will be aware of the ethical debates. To some the key point is the status of the fetus. If the fetus is a person, it has a right to life and cannot be killed. If, however, it is not a person, the fetus can be removed at the wish of the woman. Feminists argue that it is impossible to consider the issue of abortion without looking at the wider social context. Restricting women's access to abortion can be seen as a means of controlling women's lives. ▶

You should be aware of the range of views available on the issue, not just the more extreme ones. The article by Thomson (1971) is interesting because it argues that, even if one believes that the fetus is a person with a right to life, it would still be improper not to permit abortions because that would be imposing too great a burden on the woman (see Finnis (1973), for a rejection of her views). Note also the discussion in Brazier (1988) which considers whether, if the issue of whether a fetus is a person is essentially a religious one and incapable of scientific assessment, the law should 'impose' that view on pregnant women. Much controversy has greeted a paper by Giubilini and Minerva (2013) that it should be permissible for a parent to kill a child after birth, as a newborn baby did not have the defining attributes of being a person. See Herring (2012, chapter 6) for a summary of the ethical debates on abortion.

■ Regulation of pregnancy

Should the law restrict the way pregnant women behave in order to protect the fetus? There is scientific evidence that a fetus can be seriously harmed by a mother's and father's behaviour during the pregnancy. Should we restrict the rights of parents to, for example, smoke during a pregnancy? The law has generally been very reluctant to do so. The issue has most dramatically arisen in cases where a woman refuses to have a Caesarean section operation without which the fetus will die. In many cases (see e.g. *Re MB (An Adult Medical Treatment)* (1997)) the courts have concluded that the woman is not competent, and so the operation can go ahead. Where, however, she is competent, her wishes must be respected.

KEY CASE

St George's Healthcare NHS Trust v. *S* [1998] 3 All ER 673

Concerning: whether it was lawful to perform a Caesarean section operation on a woman without her consent

Facts

S was 35 weeks pregnant when she was told she needed to have a Caesarean section operation. She was told that without one she and/or the fetus would die. She refused to consent. Her doctors assessed her competent to make the decision to refuse, but sought judicial approval to perform the operation. This was given by Hogg J and a baby girl was born as a result. After the birth, the mother appealed against Hogg J's decision.

Legal principle

The Court of Appeal held that the mother's detention and the performance of the operation without her consent was unlawful. They confirmed that a competent woman had an absolute right to refuse treatment. This was not affected by the fact that she was pregnant. This was so even if without it she and the fetus would die.

■ Putting it all together

Answer guidelines

See the problem question at the start of the chapter.

Approaching the question

Sometimes the examiner sets a problem question which requires you to know about several topics to write a good answer. Don't worry about that; it gives you an opportunity to show the width of your knowledge. Here you need to show an understanding of the law on consent as well as the law on the regulation of pregnancy.

Important points to include

The first issue to be determined is whether or not Marion is competent. See the test for capacity in the Mental Capacity Act (discussed in Chapter 2). You should note the willingness of the courts in cases of this kind to find a woman in labour incompetent (see e.g. *Re MB* (1997)). But notice the warnings in *St George's* v. *S* (1998) that the courts should not find a woman incompetent simply because they find her decision irrational.

If Marion lacks capacity, the court will make a decision based on what is in her best interests (again, see Chapter 2). Note that in the case law (e.g. *Re MB*) it is generally assumed that it is in the best interests of a woman who is in the late stages of pregnancy to give birth.

If Marion has capacity, the next issue is to consider what she has decided about her treatment. Here her views appear contradictory. Note that for the doctors to perform the operation they need her consent to the operation (a lack of objection is insufficient). Consider the arguments on either side on how best to understand the woman's views here.

 Make your answer stand out

A good answer will show a good understanding of the case law on the status of the fetus. Notice, however, that the courts in *St George's* v. *S* state that the right to refuse treatment of the woman trumps any interests the fetus might have.

READ TO IMPRESS

Brazier, M. (1988) 'Embryo's "Rights": abortion and research' in M. Freeman (ed.), *Medicine, Ethics and Law*. London: Stevens.

Dworkin, R. (1993) *Life's Dominion*. London: Harper Collins.

Finnis, J. (1973) 'The Rights and Wrongs of Abortion', 2 *Philosophy and Public Affairs* 117.

Fox, M. (1998) 'A Woman's Right to Choose: a feminist critique', in J. Harris and S. Holm (eds), *The Future of Human Reproduction*. Oxford: Oxford University Press.

Giubilini, A. and Minerva, F. (2013) 'After-birth Abortion: why should the baby live?', 39 *Journal of Medical Ethics* 261.

Herring, J. (2011) 'The Loneliness of Status: the legal and moral significance of birth', in F. Ebtehaj, J. Herring, M. Johnson and M. Richards (eds), *Birth Rites and Rights*. Oxford: Hart.

Herring, J. (2012) *Medical Law and Ethics*. Oxford: Oxford University Press.

Kaczor, C. (2011) *The Ethics of Abortion*. Cambridge: Cambridge University Press.

Scott, R. (2005) 'Interpreting the Disability Ground of the Abortion Act', 64 *Cambridge Law Journal* 388.

Sifris, R. (2010) 'Restrictive Regulation of Abortion and the Right to Health', 18 *Medical Law Review* 185.

Thomson, J. J. (1971) 'A Defense of Abortion', 1 *Philosophy and Public Affairs* 1.

Tooley, M. *et al.* (2009) *Abortion: Three Perspectives*. Oxford: Oxford University Press.

www.pearsoned.co.uk/lawexpress

Go online to access more revision support including quizzes to test your knowledge, sample questions with answer guidelines, podcasts you can download, and more!

Reproduction

7

■ Topic map

Forms of
assisted
reproduction

Unlawful reproductive
activities: *R (Quintavalle)* v. *HFEA*

Regulated reproductive
activities: *Evans* v. *Amicus Healthcare*

Unregulated reproductive
activities — Who is the parent of a child?

A printable version of this topic map is available from **www.pearsoned.co.uk/lawexpress**

■ Introduction

Producing children has never been more complicated.

True, there is the ever-popular traditional method (sexual intercourse), but there is also available a range of alternatives. The law sometimes appears to have trouble keeping up with the fast pace of change in this area. There are two major issues facing the law. The first is how to regulate the reproductive services on offer. Should all kinds of reproductive service be available? And should they be open to everyone? The second is the question of who should be regarded as the parents of a child born as a result of reproductive services.

ASSESSMENT ADVICE

Essay questions

It is difficult to predict which question may be asked on this topic. There is a wide range for the examiner to choose from: access to reproductive services; issues surrounding surrogacy; embryo selection; cloning; determining parentage. All of these could be selected. However, there are some theoretical themes which run through this topic. One is the concept of reproductive autonomy. It will be very useful to be aware of this issue and the arguments for and against it. Another issue concerns the status of the embryo. The position in law appears to be that, although the embryo is not a person, it is protected to some extent by the law. If then the law recognises that the embryo has some interests, what exactly are these?

Problem questions

The most obvious area for a problem question to arise would be over the parentage of a child. You are likely to face a scenario where a number of people could claim to be the father or mother of the child. To answer such a question you will need to have a good understanding of the relevant case law and the provisions of the Human Fertilisation and Embryology Act 1990. You should note, however, that in interpreting the legislation the courts have attempted to ensure that a 'sensible' result is reached. Also, don't forget the option of adoption. So if the people actually raising the child are not in law the parents, they could apply to adopt the child and become parents that way.

■ Sample question

Could you answer this question? Below is a typical problem question that could arise on this topic. Guidelines on answering the question are included at the end of this chapter, whilst a sample essay question and guidance on tackling it can be found on the companion website.

PROBLEM QUESTION

Adam and Eve are an unmarried couple who have had trouble conceiving a child. They approach a licensed clinic for treatment. They are offered treatment using donated sperm, from Dave, and a donated egg, from Mary. During the weeks they are receiving information and tests, Adam and Eve's relationship comes to an end. However, they do not inform the clinic of this. After the breakup Eve attends the clinic alone but reassures the staff that she is still in a relationship with Adam. She then, by chance, meets and falls in love with Dave. Dave goes along with Eve to the clinic on the day the embryo is implanted. Dave and Eve marry shortly before baby Cain is born.

Who are Cain's parents?

■ Some key theoretical issues

Behind many of the issues raised in this chapter is the concept of **reproductive autonomy**.

KEY DEFINITION: Reproductive autonomy

Supporters of reproductive autonomy argue that the decisions people make about whether or not to have children are intimate and profoundly important. The state should assist couples in their choice. Where a person or a couple wishes to have a child, the state should assist them as far as is possible (given other restraints on resources). It is not the state's job to decide whether a person will make a good or bad parent or to restrict the way a person wishes to create a child. Sometimes the concept is distinguished from 'reproductive liberty' where, while the state should not prevent someone having a child, it is not under a positive obligation to assist them.

Supporters of reproductive autonomy often point out that the state does nothing to prevent people from becoming parents if they are able to have a child 'naturally'. The state does not even stop a known paedophile from fathering a child (of course, it would be difficult for it to do so). So, surely, the state should not prevent people who suffer infertility from becoming parents. Otherwise, the state will be discriminating on the grounds of disability (infertility). Opponents argue that while the state cannot prevent people from becoming parents 'naturally', it would be irresponsible to allow people whose children would suffer, to become parents.

 Make your answer stand out

In order to write a great answer, it is well worth becoming familiar with the debates over the notion of reproductive autonomy. One issue which has not been addressed sufficiently by opponents of reproductive autonomy is that if we are to restrict who can have access to reproductive services, who should make the decisions: clinicians, the HFEA, judges? Also, under the current law the cost of assisted reproductive techniques prevents many people from accessing these services: is that justifiable?

■ The different techniques of assisted reproduction

The most commons forms of reproductive techniques are as follows.

Reproductive technique	What it involves
Cryopreservation	This involves freezing sperm or ova or embryos
Assisted insemination by partner	Here the sperm of the woman's partner is placed inside her and it fertilises one of her eggs
Donor insemination	Here sperm from a donor is used and placed inside a woman to fertilise one of her eggs
In vitro fertilisation	Here eggs are removed from a woman and fertilised in a laboratory. The fertilised egg is then returned to the woman. Sperm from a partner or a donor may be used
Intracytoplasmic sperm injection	A sperm (from a partner or donor) is injected into an egg (from the woman or donated). The fertilised egg is then transferred back inside the woman

The issues raised by these different techniques vary enormously. For example, where a wife simply has her husband's sperm placed inside her, this raises few, if any, legal or ethical issues. It is where the treatment involves the sperm of a donor or the creation of embryos outside the woman that the issues become more complex.

■ The regulation of the Human Fertilisation and Embryology Authority

The Human Fertilisation and Embryology Authority (HFEA) regulates much assisted reproduction through the Human Fertilisation and Embryology Act 1990 (HFEAct).

Activities which are unlawful under the HFEAct

The HFEAct prohibits certain reproductive activities and does not permit the HFEA to license them. These are as follows.

Unlawful reproductive activity	Statutory provision
No embryo can be stored for more than 14 days after the mixing of the gametes (sperm or eggs)	HFEAct, s. 4A(3)
A non-human embryo or gamete (e.g. that of an animal) cannot be placed in a woman	HFEAct, s. 3(2)
It is unlawful to place a human embryo in an animal	HFEAct, s. 3(3)
Eggs taken from embryos cannot be used in fertility treatment	HFEAct, s. 3A
It is unlawful to alter the genetic structure of any cell which is part of an embryo	HFEAct, Sch. 2, para. 1(4)

Activities only lawful if done under a licence from HFEA

There are certain activities which are illegal unless the clinic has been licensed to do them by the HFEA. These are the following.

Activity only lawful if licensed	Statutory provision
The storage of an embryo	HFEAct, s. 41
The mixing of human and non-human gametes	HFEAct, s. 4
The storage and use of gametes	HFEAct, ss. 3 and 4

Activities which do not require a licence

There is, of course, no need to obtain a licence to engage in sexual intercourse! But nor is there any need to have a licence for so-called 'do-it-yourself insemination' if it involves live gametes and there is no storage involved.

■ Controversial issues involving assisted reproduction

Disputes over frozen embryos

What if a couple use their gametes to produce an embryo which is stored by a licensed clinic, but they split up and one of them wants the embryo destroyed and the other does not? That issue was dealt with in the following case which made it clear that the embryo had to be destroyed.

KEY CASE

Evans v. *Amicus Healthcare* [2004] 3 All ER 1025; *Evans* v. *UK* [2006] 1 FCR 585
Concerning: how to resolve disputes over frozen embryos

Facts

Natalie Evans and Howard Johnston were engaged when they underwent IVF treatment. Ms Evans was undergoing cancer treatment and they were told that they should freeze embryos because after the treatment she would be unable to have any children of her own. Six embryos were created and frozen with the intent that they would be used once Ms Evans had completed her treatment. In 2002 the couple separated and Mr Johnston asked the clinic to destroy the embryos. Ms Evans wanted to use the embryos to become pregnant. If they were destroyed, she would lose all chance of having children of her own.

Legal principle

The Court of Appeal held that under the terms of the Human Fertilisation and Embryology Act 1990 a clinic was only entitled to store an embryo if both the people who had provided the gametes which had produced the embryo consented to the embryo being stored. Once one party withdrew consent, the embryos had to be destroyed.

The Court of Appeal also held that there was nothing in the Human Rights Act 1998 which required the courts to reach a different conclusion. Ms Evans appealed ultimately to the Grand Chamber of the European Court on Human Rights. The Chamber held that the case involved a clash of Article 8 rights: Mr Johnston's right not to be a father against his wishes; and Ms Evans's right to be able to become a mother. It was up to each individual country to decide how to balance these competing rights under their 'margin of appreciation'. The choice of English law to prefer Mr Johnston's rights could not be said to be improper.

> ✎ **EXAM TIP**
>
> It is well worth having a good think about the issues raised in *Evans* v. *UK* (see Lind (2006)). Do you agree that the right not to be a parent is as important as the right to be a parent? Which would be a greater interference in how people wish to live their life: to be a parent against their wishes, or not being able to be a parent when they wish to be? Do you think the interests of the embryos should have had any role to play in the decision?

■ Restrictions to treatment

When a couple approaches a clinic for treatment, the clinic must consider whether it is appropriate to offer them treatment services. This will involve the likelihood of success. More controversial is section 13(5), HFEAct.

> **KEY STATUTE**
>
> **Human Fertilisation and Embryology Act 1990, section 13(5)**
>
> A woman shall not be provided with treatment services unless account has been taken of the welfare of any child who may be born as a result of the treatment (including the need of that child for supportive parenting), and of any other child who may be affected by the birth.

The wording of this section has been amended by the 2008 Human Fertilisation and Embryology Act. Previously the section had required the clinic to consider the need of the child for a father. As a result some clinics had not offered (or only rarely offered) services to lesbian couples or single women. As a result of the amendment, services should be available to single women or lesbian couples, as long as the clinic is persuaded the child will receive supportive parenting. Clinics might also consider the age of the parties seeking treatment. Is it appropriate to offer reproductive services to a woman who will be a pensioner when her child is a teenager?

Embryo selection

Some forms of reproductive assistance lead to the creation of several embryos; some of these will then be implanted into the woman. The clinic will normally test to see which embryos are healthy before deciding which to implant. This is not particularly controversial; much more controversial is whether other factors can be taken into account when deciding which embryos to implant. The leading case on this is the following:

KEY CASE

R (Quintavalle) v. HFEA [2005] UKHL 28

Concerning: the legality of selecting embryos for implantation

Facts

A couple had a child (Zain) who suffered a serious disability. The only hope of cure was if a sibling had stem cells which were an appropriate match. Using assisted reproductive techniques, the couple produced some embryos. They wanted to have them tested to see which (when born) could provide a suitable match for Zain. A licence was granted by the HFEA to do this. Comment on Reproductive Ethics (CORE, a pro-life pressure group) sought a judicial review of this.

Legal principle

Section 11 of the Human Fertilisation and Embryology Act 1990 allowed the HFEA to license certain activities. These included practices designed to secure that embryos are in a 'suitable condition' to be placed in a woman. Their Lordships held that 'suitable' here could mean suitable to the woman concerned. This permitted the HFEA to grant this licence.

Surrogacy

KEY DEFINITION: Surrogacy

One woman (the surrogate mother) agrees to carry a child for another woman or a couple (the commissioning couple). Their intention is that shortly after birth the child will be handed over to the commissioning couple and they will raise the child.

Surrogacy is a controversial practice. The law's response to surrogacy is somewhat ambiguous. However, it is clear that a surrogacy arrangement is unenforceable.

KEY STATUTE

Surrogacy Arrangements Act 1985, section 1A

No surrogacy arrangement is enforceable by or against any of the persons making it.

Where, therefore, the surrogate mother after birth decides that she wishes to keep the child, the commissioning couple cannot enforce the contract to hand the child over. However, they could seek a residence order under the Children Act 1989. The court would only be likely to grant this if it thought that the surrogate mother posed a risk to the child (*Re T (A Child) (Surrogacy: Residence Order)* (2011)).

If the surrogate agreement works and the child is handed over, the commissioning couple can either seek to adopt the child or seek a parental order under section 30 of the Human

Fertilisation and Embryology Act 1990 (although the criteria for obtaining one are strict). A parental order will not normally be made if substantial sums are handed over (although see *Re L (A Child)* (2010) for an indication the courts may be becoming more liberal on this).

> **✎ EXAM TIP**
>
> A popular question in the exam is whether or not surrogacy should be permitted or even encouraged in the law (see Jackson (2001)). The primary argument in favour is liberty: if all the individuals concerned are happy to enter into the contract, it should be respected and the state should not intervene. Opponents cite concerns for the well-being of any child (especially if the arrangement breaks down) and worries that a surrogacy contract is akin to slavery.

■ Parentage

Who in law is a child's parent? The general rule is that a child's mother is the mother who gave birth to the child, while the child's father is the man whose sperm fertilised the egg. Where there is any doubt over this, DNA tests can be used to establish who the father is. However, the Human Fertilisation and Embryology Acts of 1990 and 2008 make some special provisions.

Mothers

> **KEY STATUTE**
>
> **Human Fertilisation and Embryology Act 2008, section 33**
>
> The woman who is carrying or has carried a child as a result of the placing in her of an embryo or of sperm and eggs, and no other woman, is to be treated as the mother of the child.

This provision makes it clear that it is the woman who gives birth to the child who is the mother. This is so even if donated eggs were used.

Sperm donors

> **KEY STATUTE**
>
> **Human Fertilisation and Embryology Act 2008, section 41**
>
> Where the sperm of a man who had given such consent as is required by paragraph 5 of Schedule 3 to the 1990 Act (consent to use of gametes for purposes of treatment services or non-medical fertility services) was used for a purpose for which such consent was required, he is not to be treated as the father of the child.

This provision makes it clear that normally a sperm donor will not be a father of a child produced. However, this is only where the sperm is used by a licensed clinic and in accordance with his consent (*M* v. *F* (2013)). Also, under the HFEAct 2008, Schedule 6, once a child born using donated sperm reaches the age of 18, they can ask for information about the donor father. For sperm donations after April 2005, this will include information revealing the identity of the donor. The new regulations have caused a reduction in the number of donors.

✎ EXAM TIP

The issue of the anonymity of donors is a controversial one and it is worth revising the issue carefully. Consider the different human rights that could be claimed here. How important is a child's right to know their genetic origins? Is such a right enforceable if (as the evidence suggests) parents are unwilling to tell their children that they were born using donor sperm? If the sperm donor shortage continues, should donor anonymity be restored?

Husbands and partners of women receiving assisted reproductive services

KEY STATUTE

Human Fertilisation and Embryology Act 2008, sections 35, 36 and 37

35 Woman married at time of treatment

(1) If–

    (a) at the time of the placing in her of the embryo or of the sperm and eggs or of her artificial insemination, W was a party to a marriage, and

    (b) the creation of the embryo carried by her was not brought about with the sperm of the other party to the marriage,

then, subject to section 38(2) to (4), the other party to the marriage is to be treated as the father of the child unless it is shown that he did not consent to the placing in her of the embryo or the sperm and eggs or to her artificial insemination (as the case may be).

. . .

36 Treatment provided to woman where agreed fatherhood conditions apply

If no man is treated by virtue of section 35 as the father of the child and no woman is treated by virtue of section 42 as a parent of the child but–

(a) the embryo or the sperm and eggs were placed in W, or W was artificially inseminated, in the course of treatment services provided in the United Kingdom by a person to whom a licence applies, ▶

(b) at the time when the embryo or the sperm and eggs were placed in W, or W was artificially inseminated, the agreed fatherhood conditions (as set out in section 37) were satisfied in relation to a man, in relation to treatment provided to W under the licence,

(c) the man remained alive at that time, and

(d) the creation of the embryo carried by W was not brought about with the man's sperm, then, subject to section 38(2) to (4), the man is to be treated as the father of the child.

37 The agreed fatherhood conditions

(1) The agreed fatherhood conditions referred to in section 36(b) are met in relation to a man ('M') in relation to treatment provided to W under a licence if, but only if,–

(a) M has given the person responsible a notice stating that he consents to being treated as the father of any child resulting from treatment provided to W under the licence,

(b) W has given the person responsible a notice stating that she consents to M being so treated,

(c) neither M nor W has, since giving notice under paragraph (a) or (b), given the person responsible notice of the withdrawal of M's or W's consent to M being so treated,

(d) W has not, since the giving of the notice under paragraph (b), given the person responsible–

(i) a further notice under that paragraph stating that she consents to another man being treated as the father of any resulting child, or

(ii) a notice under section 44(1)(b) stating that she consents to a woman being treated as a parent of any resulting child, and

(e) W and M are not within prohibited degrees of relationship in relation to each other.

(2) A notice under subsection (1)(a), (b) or (c) must be in writing and must be signed by the person giving it.

(3) A notice under subsection (1)(a), (b) or (c) by a person ('S') who is unable to sign because of illness, injury or physical disability is to be taken to comply with the requirement of subsection (2) as to signature if it is signed at the direction of S, in the presence of S and in the presence of at least one witness who attests the signature.

In short, if a woman has received treatment at a licensed clinic using donated sperm, then her husband will be treated as the father of any child born, unless he can show that he did not consent. A woman's unmarried male partner can be treated as the father of any child born if he has consented to be treated as such.

The 2008 Human Fertilisation and Embryology Act has enabled female cohabitants and civil partners of a mother to be a parent of a child.

KEY STATUTE

Human Fertilisation and Embryology Act 2008, sections 42, 43 and 44

42 Woman in civil partnership at time of treatment

(1) If at the time of the placing in her of the embryo or the sperm and eggs or of her artificial insemination, W was a party to a civil partnership, then subject to section 45(2) to (4), the other party to the civil partnership is to be treated as a parent of the child unless it is shown that she did not consent to the placing in W of the embryo or the sperm and eggs or to her artificial insemination (as the case may be).

(2) This section applies whether W was in the United Kingdom or elsewhere at the time mentioned in subsection (1).

43 Treatment provided to woman who agrees that second woman to be parent

If no man is treated by virtue of section 35 as the father of the child and no woman is treated by virtue of section 42 as a parent of the child but–

(a) the embryo or the sperm and eggs were placed in W, or W was artificially inseminated, in the course of treatment services provided in the United Kingdom by a person to whom a licence applies,

(b) at the time when the embryo or the sperm and eggs were placed in W, or W was artificially inseminated, the agreed female parenthood conditions (as set out in section 44) were met in relation to another woman, in relation to treatment provided to W under that licence, and

(c) the other woman remained alive at that time, then, subject to section 45(2) to (4), the other woman is to be treated as a parent of the child.

44 The agreed female parenthood conditions

(1) The agreed female parenthood conditions referred to in section 43(b) are met in relation to another woman ('P') in relation to treatment provided to W under a licence if, but only if,–

 (a) P has given the person responsible a notice stating that P consents to P being treated as a parent of any child resulting from treatment provided to W under the licence,

 (b) W has given the person responsible a notice stating that W agrees to P being so treated,

 (c) neither W nor P has, since giving notice under paragraph (a) or (b), given the person responsible notice of the withdrawal of P's or W's consent to P being so treated,

 (d) W has not, since the giving of the notice under paragraph (b), given the person responsible–

  (i) a further notice under that paragraph stating that W consents to a woman other than P being treated as a parent of any resulting child, or

  (ii) a notice under section 37(1)(b) stating that W consents to a man being treated as the father of any resulting child, and

▶

> (e) W and P are not within prohibited degrees of relationship in relation to each other.
> (2) A notice under subsection (1)(a), (b) or (c) must be in writing and must be signed by the person giving it.
> (3) A notice under subsection (1)(a), (b) or (c) by a person ('S') who is unable to sign because of illness, injury or physical disability is to be taken to comply with the requirement of subsection (2) as to signature if it is signed at the direction of S, in the presence of S and in the presence of at least one witness who attests the signature.

This statute, therefore, enables the civil partner of the mother, or her female cohabitant to be recognised as a parent of a child. This means that there is no discrimination between a woman who is receiving licensed treatment with a male partner, and a female partner.

✓ Make your answer stand out

In your essays make sure you include the law's approach to parenthood where a lesbian couple have a child. When Parliament discussed the 2008 Human Fertilisation and Embryology Act there was much debate over what name to give the female partner of the child. Should she be called a mother, in which case the child would have two mothers? Although this might seem to be the most natural solution, it was rejected by Parliament, which preferred the title of 'second parent'. Is this a fixation with an out-of-date understanding of what parenthood is about? Or should the title 'mother' be restricted to the woman who actually carries the child through pregnancy and gives birth?

■ Putting it all together

Answer guidelines

See the problem question at the start of the chapter.

Approaching the question

This question focuses on deciding who the parents of the child are. Don't be tempted to stray into other issues you think are interesting. Focus on the question asked.

Important points to include

The key issues raised in this problem question are as follows:

- Is Eve the mother of the child? See section 33 of the HFEAct 2008.
- Is Adam the father by virtue of section 37? Note the formalities that would need to be gone through if this is to be satisfied.
- Can Dave be regarded as the father of the child? Note: as the husband of a woman who gives birth, he will be presumed to be the father. But will section 41 mean he is not if his paternity is challenged? If he is not, who will be?

READ TO IMPRESS

Alghrani, A. and Harris, J. (2007) 'Reproductive Liberty: should the foundation of families be regulated?', 18 *Child and Family Law Quarterly* 191.

Donchin, A. (2011) 'In Whose Interest? Policy and Politics in Assisted Reproduction', 25 *Bioethics* 92.

Hammond, J. (2010) 'Genetic Engineering to Avoid Genetic Neglect: from chance to responsibility', 24 *Bioethics* 10.

Harris, J. (2005) 'No Sex Selection Please, We're British', 31 *Journal of Medical Ethics* 286.

Harris, J. and Holm, S. (2004) *The Future of Reproduction*. Oxford: Oxford University Press.

Horsey, K. (2011) 'Challenging Presumptions: legal parenthood and surrogacy arrangements', 22 *Child and Family Law Quarterly* 449.

Jackson, E. (2008) 'Degendering Reproduction', 16 *Medical Law Review* 346.

Lind, C. (2006) '*Evans v United Kingdom*: judgments of Solomon: power, gender and procreation', 18 *Child and Family Law Quarterly* 576.

Scott, R. (2006) 'Choosing between Possible Lives: legal and ethics issues in pre-implantation genetic diagnosis', 26 *Oxford Journal of Legal Studies* 153.

www.pearsoned.co.uk/lawexpress

Go online to access more revision support including quizzes to test your knowledge, sample questions with answer guidelines, podcasts you can download, and more!

Organd donation and ownership of body parts

8

■ Topic map

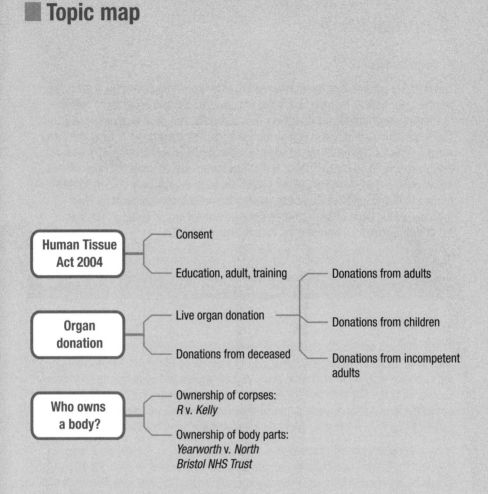

Human Tissue Act 2004
- Consent
- Education, adult, training

Organ donation
- Live organ donation
- Donations from deceased
  - Donations from adults
  - Donations from children
  - Donations from incompetent adults

Who owns a body?
- Ownership of corpses: *R* v. *Kelly*
- Ownership of body parts: *Yearworth* v. *North Bristol NHS Trust*

■ Introduction

Is your body yours?

You probably assume it is, but the law on this is far from straightforward. It is unclear whether your body is property and, if so, who owns it. And this is not just a question of interest to high-minded philosophers. Human bodies can be of huge financial value. There is a serious shortage of organs for donations. The current law is fairly strict over when a person's organs should be used for transplantation and some people believe the law should be liberalised. There is also increasing awareness of the value of an individual's DNA, especially when it can be used to develop new drug treatments. At the same time, great public outcry greeted the news that hospitals have been routinely storing parts of dead children's bodies without proper consent. This has led to a change in the law under the Human Tissue Act 2004.

ASSESSMENT ADVICE

Essay questions

These may well ask you to consider the recently passed Human Tissue Act 2004. You need to be aware of the scandals which led to the passing of the Act. This helps explain the extensive regulation which is in place. A good answer will demonstrate an excellent knowledge of the Act. Note that the Act does not take the simple approach of saying that consent is required for any use of human tissue. You will need to consider when human tissue can be used without consent and whether these exceptions are ever justified.

Another popular topic with examiners is organ transplantation. You will need to be aware of the current law, but also the intense debates over how, if at all, the law should be reformed. A final issue which you may be asked to write about is whether the body is property and, if so, who owns it. A good answer will not just deal with this as an abstract legal or philosophical question but also consider specific areas where it might matter what the legal status of the body is.

Problem questions

These are likely to require a detailed knowledge of the Human Tissue Act 2004. Make a careful note of what the consequence is of breaching the provisions of the Act. Notice that sometimes a criminal conviction is possible, other times just a claim in tort; and for some it is unclear what the punishment is. A problem question could also arise over an organ donation, particularly involving a clash between the wishes of the deceased and relatives. You will need a clear understanding of how such clashes of wish are resolved.

■ Sample question

Could you answer this question? Below is a typical essay question that could arise on this topic. Guidelines on answering the question are included at the end of this chapter, whilst a sample problem question and guidance on tackling it can be found on the companion website.

ESSAY QUESTION

To what extent are the wishes of the deceased respected in the law on organ transplantation? To what extent should they be?

■ The Human Tissue Act 2004

The Act is designed to provide a detailed framework for issues relating to the taking, storage and use of human organs and tissue. However, you should realise that it does not cover all dealings with human body parts. In particular, it does not deal with the following.

- The removal of materials from humans. The Act covers the use or storage of removed material but has nothing to say about when it is lawful to actually remove the material from a body.
- The Act does not deal with eggs, sperm or human embryos.
- The Act only deals with the storage and use of human materials for the purposes listed in Schedule 1 to the Act (these include medical research or transplantation). They do not include, for example, the storage or taking of materials for artistic purposes or curiosity.

KEY DEFINITION: Relevant material

The HTA 2004 only covers the use and storage of 'relevant material'. This is tissue, cells and organs of human beings. It does not include sperm, eggs or embryos. Cell lines or other human material created in a laboratory are not covered.

 Make your answer stand out

Knowledge of the background behind the Human Tissue Act will impress the examiners. The Human Tissue Act 2004 was passed following a series of scandals at hospitals (most famously at Alder Hay) where tissue and organs were removed from ▶

dead children, without the consent of the parents, and the parents were not informed of it. When what had happened was discovered, many parents were horrified. (See Price (2005) for a summary of the background to the Act.) It is interesting to note that, while the Act tightens up the regulation of the storage of tissue and organs, it is permissible in some circumstances to store a person's tissue without consent.

The central provision in the 2004 Human Tissue Act is section 1.

KEY STATUTE

Human Tissue Act 2004, section 1(1)

The following activities shall be lawful if done with appropriate consent –

(a) the storage of the body of a deceased person for use for a purpose specified in Schedule 1, other than anatomical examination;

(b) the use of the body of a deceased person for a purpose so specified, other than anatomical examination;

(c) the removal from the body of a deceased person, for use for a purpose specified in Schedule 1, of any relevant material of which the body consists or which it contains;

(d) the storage for use for a purpose specified in Part 1 of Schedule 1 of any relevant material which has come from a human body;

(e) the storage for use for a purpose specified in Part 2 of Schedule 1 of any relevant material which has come from the body of a deceased person;

(f) the use for a purpose specified in Part 1 of Schedule 1 of any relevant material which has come from a human body;

(g) the use for a purpose specified in Part 2 of Schedule 1 of any relevant material which has come from the body of a deceased person.

❗ Don't be tempted to . . .

It is easy to make the mistake of thinking that if section 1 is breached a legal wrong is clearly committed. Although section 1 makes it clear what medical professionals must do if they are to act lawfully, the statute does not make it clear what the legal consequences are if a professional does not meet the requirements in section 1. It may be that an offence of theft will be committed or perhaps a tortious wrong. Just possibly there is a gap in the legislation and no wrong is committed at all.

Section 1 sets out when it is lawful to deal with certain bodily materials. It must be shown that the activity was done with the necessary consent and for a 'Schedule 1 purpose'. You need to be familiar with these terms.

Consent

If one of the activities mentioned in section 1 is done without consent, it can amount to a crime (see HTA, section 5). Whether or not there has been the necessary consent all depends on the category of person involved.

Alive adult

The normal law of consent applies (see Chapter 3). So an adult with capacity and appropriately informed can give consent to the use or storage of their bodily material.

Deceased adults

If the deceased has made their views clear these must be followed. If the person died without expressing a view about what should happen to their body but appointed a representative to make such decisions, then the representative's views will be followed. If there is no appointed representative, then the closest 'qualifying relative' can make the decision (see HTA, section 27(4) for the list of qualifying relatives).

Children

If children are competent, they can make any decisions about the use or storage of their bodily material. If not, then a person with parental responsibility can make the decision.

Incapacitated adults

Under the Human Tissue Act 2004 (Persons who Lack Capacity to Consent and Transplants) Regulations 2006 there is deemed consent to store and use material from adults who lack capacity in certain circumstances. These include: where the material is for use in an authorised clinical trial; or where the use or storage would be in the incompetent person's best interests.

Schedule 1 purposes

Section 1 of the Human Tissue Act only renders an act lawful if you are acting for a Schedule 1 purpose. If you are not provided a statute book in the exam, you should try and remember some of the purposes in the Schedule by way of example. Part 1 of Schedule 1 includes transplantation and public display; Part 2 includes clinical audit or education and training.

> ✎ **EXAM TIP**
>
> An important point to make when discussing the Human Tissue Act in the exam is that there are a number of exceptions to the principle that it is not permissible to store and use human material without a person's consent. These include: where the material is stored for education, training or audit; where a High Court has made an order permitting the use of bodily material for medical research; where the Human Tissue Authority has deemed consent because it is not possible to trace the person from whom the material originated; and where the material has been imported from overseas. You should reflect on whether you think these are good enough reasons to depart from the normal principle that consent is required.

◼ Transplanting organs

The technological advances which have meant that an organ can be taken from one person and transplanted into another are exciting and literally life-saving for some. The legal regulation of organ donation varies between living adult donors, living child donors and deceased donors.

Living adult donors

There are no special legal problems about the donation of **regenerative bodily material** such as blood or bone marrow. As long as there is consent in line with the general law of consent (see Chapter 3), this is permissible. The difficulty is with donation of non-regenerative material, such as a kidney or liver.

> **KEY DEFINITION: Regenerative bodily material**
>
> This is bodily material which (if taken from a body) will be naturally replaced by the body. Blood or bone marrow would be good examples. Non-regenerative material will not be replaced by the body. Examples would be a heart or kidney.

The law does not permit a person to donate an organ if that would cause their death or serious harm. Donation of a single kidney or a segment of a liver may be permissible, but not donation of a heart! The procedure must be consented to by the donor. Finally, the requirement of section 33 of the HTA must be complied with.

> **KEY STATUTE**
>
> **Human Tissue Act 2004, section 33**
>
> (1) Subject to subsections (3) and (5), a person commits an offence if –
>
>   (a) he removes any transplantable material from the body of a living person intending that the material be used for the purpose of transplantation, and
>
>   (b) when he removes the material, he knows or might reasonably be expected to know, that the person from whose body he removes the material is alive.
>
> (2) Subject to subsections (3) and (5), a person commits an offence if –
>
>   (a) he uses for the purposes of transplantation any transplantable material which has come from the body of a living person, and
>
>   (b) when he does so, he knows, or might reasonably be expected to know, that the transplantable material has come from the body of a living person.

> (3) The Secretary of State may by regulations provide that subsection (1) or (2) shall not apply in a case where –
>
>   (a) the Authority is satisfied –
>
>   (i) that no reward has been or is to be given in contravention of section 32, and
>
>   (ii) that such other conditions as are specified in the regulations are satisfied, and
>
>   (b) such other requirements as are specified in the regulations are complied with.

The guidance issued by the Human Tissue Authority (2006) requires that the proposed donor be given extensive information about the procedure. Where the donor is not genetically or emotionally linked with the recipient, the donor needs to have a meeting with a clinician and an independent assessor and then the donation needs the approval of the Authority.

Children donating

There is little clear guidance on the legal position where children are donating organs. The Human Tissue Authority (2006) has stated that only very rarely will living donations from children be acceptable. If the child is not competent, it might be argued that parents cannot consent to a donation on behalf of a child except in the rare cases when such a donation will be in the interests of a child. Where the child is competent, it may well be that the child can then consent. However, it may be rare that a child would have sufficient understanding to be competent (as was suggested by Lord Donaldson in *Re W (A Minor) (Medical Treatment)* (1992).

An incompetent adult

It is not clear whether an incompetent adult could be taken to consent. It would need to be shown that the donation was in the best interests of the incompetent person. This might be possible if the donation was to someone close to the incompetent person (see e.g. *Re Y* (1997)).

Transplants from the dead

The law regulating transplants from the dead is covered by the Human Tissue Act 2004 and the general principle is that organs can only be removed from a dead person with 'appropriate consent'. The key issue is whether there is 'appropriate consent'. As we saw above, this means first asking whether or not the deceased had made a decision about organ transplantation on death (e.g. had they signed an organ donor card?). If not, then the question is whether they have nominated a representative and, if not, then the person who is the closest qualifying relative can make the decision.

The list of who makes the decision about donation in order of priority	Section of the HTA 2004
The deceased	s. 1
The person appointed by the deceased as their representative	s. 3
Spouse or partner	s. 27
Parent or child	s. 27
Brother or sister	s. 27
Grandparent or grandchild	s. 27
Child of brother or sister	s. 27
Stepfather or stepmother	s. 27
Half-brother or half-sister	s. 27
Friend of long standing	s. 27

✓ Make your answer stand out

In an essay on organ donation you should show a good knowledge of the arguments surrounding the current law. There has been much debate over whether or not the current law on organ donation is appropriate. Some argue that we should have an 'opt out' system. This would mean that the presumption would be that people would want to donate their organs for transplantation, unless they made it clear they did not. Under the current system, a person or that person's relatives have to positively choose that they do want to donate, if transplantation is to be lawful. Supporters of an 'opt out' system argue that it is reasonable to assume that people would want to help others. Opponents argue that you cannot do anything to a person's body without their consent.

■ The body as property

The question of whether we own our own bodies is not just of philosophical interest. It is of practical legal importance. The traditional approach of the law has been that the body is not property. This means that a person cannot sell their organs (see Human Tissue Act 2004, section 32, which makes it an offence to deal with organs for reward). However, in more recent years, the law has been more open to the idea that in some circumstances a body might become property (see R v. Kelly (1998)). The leading case is now the following.

KEY CASE

Yearworth v. *North Bristol NHS Trust* **[2009] EWCA Civ 37**

Concerning: ownership of body parts

Facts

Six men who were due to receive chemotherapy which could have rendered them infertile, chose to store their sperm at the hospital. The hospital negligently failed to store the sperm properly and it was useless. The men suffered emotional distress as a result. Fortunately none of them was in fact rendered infertile by the chemotherapy.

Legal principle

No personal injury claim could be brought as the sperm was no longer part of their body. However, the Court of Appeal was willing to recognise that the sperm was property belonging to the men. Under the law of bailment the court was willing to grant damages to the men, who were said to have given their property to the hospital to look after.

! Don't be tempted to . . .

The law on ownership of bodies is still very unclear and you should not pretend that the law is now certain. It is still far from clear when bodies become property. In *Kelly* it was said that a corpse could become property if skill was applied to it. In *Yearworth* the Court of Appeal gave four reasons why the sperm was their property:

1 The men's body had created the sperm.

2 The sole purpose of creating the sperm was for the men's future use.

3 Under the Human Fertilisation and Embryology Act 1990 the hospital had duties to store the sperm properly.

4 No one else had any claim to the sperm.

It is unclear how the law will develop in this area. In *Moore* v. *Regents of the University of California* (1990) the American courts had to deal with a case where parts of a man's body (which contained useful genetic material) were used to develop a drug which made millions of dollars for the drug company. The question was whether the man was entitled to claim that the product was generated by him and, therefore, he was entitled to at least a share in the profits. The American courts thought not, but the issues will be before the English courts soon, too, no doubt.

■ Putting it all together

Answer guidelines

See the essay question at the start of the chapter.

Approaching the question

Notice that this question asks you what the law is and what you think the law should be. Remember to address both issues. You might spend a little more time on one as compared with the other, but make sure you discuss each issue properly.

Important points to include

You will want to set out clearly when the law permits the organs of a deceased person to be used in organ transplantation. Notice that if the deceased has made it clear that they do want their organs to be used for transplantation, then their relatives have no legal basis to object. However, in practice, a doctor may decide not to use a deceased's organs if the relatives strongly object to their use.

On the ethical issue, there are some who argue that once a person has died the person has no legitimate say over what should happen to their body and so the person's wishes should be irrelevant. You could discuss whether a person owns their body (*Yearworth* v. *North Bristol NHS Trust*). Others argue that the relatives have little claim over what happens to the body of a deceased person. Any claim they may have is weaker than that of people who need an organ transplant if they are to live (see Wilkinson (2003) for further discussion).

✓   Make your answer stand out

A good answer will bring out some of the issues about ownership of our bodies. What interests do we have in our bodies? (see Wall (2011)). Do the kinds of interests we have in our body disappear on death or do they carry on?

READ TO IMPRESS

Chau, P.-L. and Herring, J. (2007) 'My Body, Your Body, Our Bodies', 15 *Medical Law Review* 34.

Cronin, A. and Harris, J. (2010) 'Authorisation, Altruism and Compulsion in the Organ Donation Debate', 36 *Journal of Medical Ethics* 627.

Herring, J. and Chau, P-L. (2013) 'Interconnected, Inhabited and Insecure: why bodies should not be property', *Journal of Medical Ethics* online.

Human Tissue Authority (2009) *Code of Practice on Consent.* London: HTA.

Laurie, G. and Harmon, S. (2010) 'Yearworth v North Bristol NHS Trust: property, principles, precedents and paradigms', 69 *Cambridge Law Journal* 476.

Nwabueze, R. (2008) 'Donated Organs, Property Rights and the Remedial Quagmire', 16 *Medical Law Review* 201.

Pattinson, S. (2011) 'Directed Donation and Ownership of Human Organs', 31 *Legal Studies* 322.

Price, D. (2005) 'The Human Tissue Act 2004', 68 *Modern Law Review* 798.

Price, D. (2009) *Human Tissue in Transplantation and Research: A Model Legal and Ethical Donation Framework.* Cambridge: Cambridge University Press.

Skeane, L. (2002) 'Proprietary Rights in Human Bodies, Body Parts and Tissue', 22 *Legal Studies* 102.

Wall, J. (2011) 'The Legal Status of Body Parts: a framework', 31 *Oxford Journal of Legal Studies* 625.

Wilkinson, S. (2003) *Bodies for Sale.* London: Routledge.

www.pearsoned.co.uk/lawexpress

Go online to access more revision support including quizzes to test your knowledge, sample questions with answer guidelines, podcasts you can download, and more!

Death and dying

9

Revision checklist

Essential points you should know:

- ☐ The legal definition of death
- ☐ The criminal law governing murder, manslaughter and suicide
- ☐ The ethical issues surrounding euthanasia, assisted suicide and death
- ☐ The legal and ethical issues surrounding refusal of treatment
- ☐ The potential significance of the Human Rights Act 1998

■ Topic map

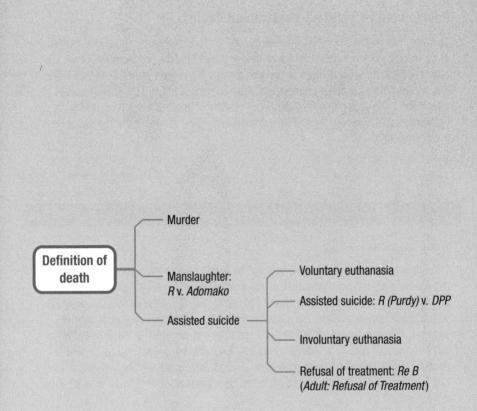

Definition of death

- Murder
- Manslaughter: *R* v. *Adomako*
- Assisted suicide
  - Voluntary euthanasia
  - Assisted suicide: *R (Purdy)* v. *DPP*
  - Involuntary euthanasia
  - Refusal of treatment: *Re B* (*Adult: Refusal of Treatment*)

■ Introduction

People hold very strong views about death.

To some, the law must protect the sanctity of life. To allow people to kill themselves or be killed by doctors shows a lack of proper respect for the preciousness of life. To others, people must be allowed to die with dignity. If a person wants to end their life, it is no one else's business to prevent it. After all, whose life is it? The law appears to take a strict line prohibiting the intentional causing of another's death or assistance in their suicide. However, behind this straightforward statement of the law lies a host of uncertainties.

ASSESSMENT ADVICE

Essay questions

There is a wide range of essays that could be asked on this topic. It is unlikely you will get one as clear-cut as: 'Does the law allow euthanasia? Should it?'; it is more likely the examiners will ask you to focus on a particular aspect of the debate. For example, you might be asked whether the significance the law attaches to the distinction between acts and omissions is justified in this context; or whether the Human Rights Act 1998 should require a change in the law. Examiners will want you to be able to explain clearly what the law is, as well as discuss what you think the law should be. Made it clear in your essay whether you are discussing what the law is, or what you think it should be.

Problem questions

These tend to focus on issues surrounding murder, manslaughter and assisted suicide. Remember to cover both the *actus reus* of the crime (e.g. did the doctor cause the death?) and the *mens rea* (e.g. did the doctor intend to kill or cause grievous bodily harm?). Unless the examiner asks you to do so in a problem question, you should be telling the examiner how the law would respond to the case, rather than discussing what you think the law should be. You may end up with the legal answer you strongly disagree with, but do not go off on a rant about it!

■ Sample question

Could you answer this question? Below is a typical essay question that could arise on this topic. Guidelines on answering the question are included at the end of this chapter, whilst a sample problem question and guidance on tackling it can be found on the companion website.

ESSAY QUESTION

Does the law allow a doctor to hasten the death of a patient? Would it be justifiable for the law to be changed to permit assisted suicide but not euthanasia?

■ The definition of death

In most cases, there is no difficulty in deciding whether someone is dead or not. But in cases where a patient is in a coma or a similar state, the question becomes tricky. The issue can be of enormous practical significance in relation to organ donation. If a person's organs are available for donation, they need to be removed at an early stage; but legally they cannot be removed before a person is dead. Indeed, there has been a suspicion that some doctors wish to define death not on the basis of when a person is truly dead, but at the time which is most convenient for organ transplant. The courts have taken the view that medicine should define death. Doctors in the UK rely on brain-stem death. It is explained that when the brain-stem has died, the person ceases to have any meaningful brain activity.

✓ Make your answer stand out

When writing about the definition of death ask yourself, why does it matter when death occurs? If a person is about to die anyway, what is so very wrong in removing their organs shortly before death? Is it possible to define death or is it better to see death as a process (see Chau and Herring (2007))? Some critics of brain-stem death claim this elevates the brain to being the only organ of significance in the body. If a person's heart is still beating and their body is still working, should the fact that their brain has ceased to function be of any relevance?

◼ Criminal law and the ending of life

A healthcare professional whose acts or omissions could cause or are connected to the death of a patient could face a number of criminal charges, most significantly:

- ◼ murder
- ◼ manslaughter
- ◼ aiding and abetting suicide.

Murder

There are two main issues which can arise in the case of a murder charge. The first is the issue of causation. Some cases have turned on whether the drugs the doctors administered killed the patient, or whether the patient died from natural causes. There can only be a murder conviction if the jury are convinced beyond reasonable doubt that the defendant caused the death of the deceased. The courts have made it clear that even if the doctor has hastened the death by a few hours, this will still amount to having caused the death of the patient (*R* v. *Arthur* (1981)). There is also some suggestion in the case law that, if the doctor is providing the standard treatment for the defendant's condition, this cannot be said to cause the patient's death (see the discussion in Biggs (2001)), although it is not quite clear what this means.

The second is the need to show intention. There are two kinds of intention recognised in the law:

- ◼ **Direct intention.** This is where it was the defendant's purpose or aim to kill the patient.
- ◼ **Indirect intention.** Here, if the defendant realised that death or grievous bodily harm was virtually certain to result from the act, then the jury are entitled to find that there was intention (*R* v. *Woollin* (1999)).

Indirect intention is very important in medical cases. Imagine that a patient is suffering from a terminal illness and a doctor administers a pain-relieving drug which the doctor knows will hasten the death of the patient. It seems that technically this could be said to amount to indirect intention (it is not direct intention as the purpose was to relieve pain not cause death). However, it is very unlikely that a jury would decide to find that this was intention. Indeed, the jury might be directed by the judge not to find intention. The law does not recognise a defence of mercy killing (*R* v. *Inglis* (2010)). Nor as the following case establishes will the courts develop the defence of necessity to cover mercy killing.

KEY CASE

R (Nicklinson) v. *Ministry of Justice* **[2013] EWCA Civ 961**

Concerning: whether the defence of necessity could apply to a case of euthanasia

Facts

Three appellants were suffering severe physical disabilities and wished to die. Their disabilities meant they could not easily kill themselves. They sought a declaration that it would be lawful for a doctor or relative to kill them relying on the defence of necessity. Failing that, they sought a declaration that the criminal law infringed their human rights.

Legal principle

The current law was clear. It was unlawful for one person to kill another unless an established defence such as self-defence applied. It would be wrong for the courts to develop the defence of necessity to apply to euthanasia cases. The issue of euthanasia was controversial and if the law was to be changed it should be done through Parliament, not the courts. There was no right to commit suicide and the current law was compliant with human rights.

! Don't be tempted to . . .

The idea of indirect intention can cause students problems and they can get it wrong. Note the following points:

- The law is clear that a jury may (but do not have to) find intention where death is foreseen as a virtually certainty.

- If a doctor sees a patient in terrible pain and so gives the patient a lethal injection in order to end the misery, this will be a case of direct intention. This is because it is part of the doctor's aim or purpose to kill the patient. This is, therefore, subtly different from where the injection is given in order to relieve pain, although it is known that as a side consequence the patient will die.

Cases of omission causing death

If death follows an omission by a doctor or healthcare professional, a murder charge can be brought. However, there are two special points to make here.

- Where a patient is incompetent, a doctor must give a patient the treatment which is in the patient's best interests. However, a doctor is not required to give treatment which is not positively in the patient's best interests. Sometimes this means that even life-saving treatment need not be given.

■ Where a patient is competent and has said that treatment may not be given, then it would be unlawful for the doctor to give the patient that treatment. This is so even where the patient is refusing life-saving treatment.

These points are illustrated by the following two cases.

KEY CASE

Airedale National Health Service Trust v. *Bland* [1993] AC 789

Concerning: the legality of withdrawing treatment from a patient in a persistent vegetative state

Facts

Tony Bland had been in a coma for over three years and was in a persistent vegetative state. His medical team, with the support of his family, sought authorisation from the courts to switch off his life-support machine and to cease providing nutrition and hydration.

Legal principle

The House of Lords emphasised that although Tony Bland was in a vegetative state, he was still alive. It was reasoned that withdrawing the treatment would be an omission, rather than an act. However, the omission would not breach the duty the doctors owed to him. This was because they were only required to provide treatment which was in the best interests of the patient. Giving him the treatment was not in his interests (nor was it against them).

EXAM TIP

It is important to note that *Bland* was decided before the Human Rights Act. There had been some discussion over whether the protection of the right to life in Article 2 and right to protection from torture and inhuman or degrading treatment in Article 3 could be used to reverse the *Bland* approach. However, Butler-Sloss P held that *Bland* was still good law even after the passing of the Human Rights Act (*NHS Trust A* v. *M* (2001)) because a withdrawal of treatment did not infringe Article 2.

KEY CASE

Re B (Adult: Refusal of Medical Treatment) [2002] 2 FCR 1

Concerning: when a competent adult can refuse treatment

Facts

Ms B, aged 41, suffered paralysis from the neck down. She was dependent on a ventilator. She asked for the ventilator to be switched off, even though she knew that without it she would die. The medical team accepted that Ms B was competent, but felt unable to comply with her wishes, believing that she still had a valuable life.

Legal principle

A competent adult has an absolute right to refuse treatment. The fact that the medical team thought her decision was contrary to her best interests was irrelevant. In this case, Ms B was competent and was aware of the relevant information and knew of the alternative options. Her decision had to be respected and the ventilator was switched off.

Following the Mental Capacity Act 2005 a patient can sign an 'advance decision' to refuse life-sustaining treatment (*X Primary Care Trust* v. *XB* (2012)). Section 25 states that such a direction has to be in writing, signed and witnessed. It is not possible to use an advance decision to ask for life-shortening treatment to be given.

> **✎ EXAM TIP**
>
> When discussing issues surrounding euthanasia, it is easy to focus on cases where a doctor causes the death of a patient. Remember that the issue can also arise where a patient is being cared for at home and a family member decides to kill the patient. When such cases are prosecuted, there is no defence of 'mercy killing' and relatives are often convicted of murder or manslaughter. In many cases where the defendant has been able to show they have been made ill by the struggles of caring for the patient, they have been able to rely on the defence of diminished responsibility. Then the sentences are often very low (e.g. *R* v. *Marshall* (2001). In other cases, the police decide that it is not in the public interest to prosecute.

Manslaughter

Where the defendant did not intend to kill or cause grievous bodily harm to the patient, a manslaughter conviction may be appropriate. This is suitable where a healthcare professional has killed a patient through extreme carelessness. In cases of that kind, the courts rely on 'gross negligence manslaughter'. As well as showing that the professional caused the death of the patient through a negligent act, the jury needs to be persuaded that the breach was bad enough to justify a conviction in criminal law, rather than just a liability to pay damages (*R* v. *Adomako* (1995)).

> **📖 REVISION NOTE**
>
> Don't forget that where a healthcare professional has caused the death of a patient through carelessness there are two possible legal consequences. The professional could be sued in the tort of negligence and be required to pay damages (see Chapter 5), and/or the professional could be prosecuted for the offence of manslaughter.

Suicide

It is not a criminal offence to commit suicide or attempt suicide. However, it is an offence to help someone else to commit suicide.

Suicide Act 1961, section 2(1)

A person who aids, abets, counsels or procures the suicide of another, or an attempt by another to commit suicide, shall be liable on conviction on indictment to imprisonment for a term not exceeding 14 years.

R (Pretty) v. *DPP* [2002] 1 AC 800; *Pretty* v. *UK* [2002] 2 FCR 97

Concerning: whether a person had a human right to be permitted to be killed or helped to commit suicide

Facts

Diane Pretty was suffering from motor neuron disease. She wanted the Director of Public Prosecutions to declare that if her husband helped her to commit suicide, he would not be prosecuted for assisting a suicide. The Director refused. She challenged his decision in the courts and the case went to the House of Lords and then the European Court of Human Rights. She claimed that English law in this area failed to adequately protect her human rights.

Legal principle

The House of Lords held that the law on assisted suicide was clear and the Director of Public Prosecutions had no power to issue an immunity from prosecution. As to the human rights issues, both the House of Lords and the European Court of Human Rights agreed that there was no right under the European Convention on Human Rights to be killed or to be helped to commit suicide. Indeed, the right to life under Article 2 indicated the state had an obligation to protect life.

R (Purdy) v. *DPP* [2009] UKHL 45

Concerning: whether the law on assisting suicide was sufficiently clear

Facts

Debbie Purdy suffered from multiple sclerosis. She foresaw a time when she would want to commit suicide. Due to her condition she would need the help of her husband to do this. If he helped her to commit suicide he could be prosecuted for the offence of assisting suicide. Under the Suicide Act 1961 the Director of Public Prosecutions (DPP) had a discretion to decide whether or not to prosecute. Ms Purdy claimed it was insufficiently clear when or how that discretion would be used.

Legal principle

The House of Lords decided that a person's decision to end their life fell within Article 8 of the ECHR. The law could justifiably interfere in that decision by making it an offence if necessary to protect the vulnerable. However, the law had to be clear. Their Lordships agreed with Ms Purdy that it was insufficiently clear when the DPP would prosecute. He was ordered to produce clearer guidelines on how he would exercise his discretion.

As a result of this decision the DPP has issued clearer guidance on when he will prosecute people for assisting suicide. Factors to be taken into account include whether the person assisting was motivated by compassion; how ill the would-be suicide was; and whether the assister would gain financially from the death. In *R (Nicklinson)* v. *Ministry of Justice* (2013) the Court of Appeal said that the guidance as it applied to medical professionals had to be made clearer.

■ Human rights and death

In *R (Pretty)* v. *DPP*; *Pretty* v. *UK* (2002) and *R (Purdy)* v. *DPP* (2009) the House of Lords and ECtHR considered the potential relevance of the ECHR and made the following points.

- **Article 2:** the right to life. This could not be interpreted to include a right to control the manner of your death.

- **Article 3:** the right not to suffer torture or inhuman and degrading treatment. The ECtHR held that even if her medical condition amounted to inhuman or degrading treatment, it could not be said that the state was inflicting that. In any event the fact that the state was required to protect the right to life under Article 2 meant that Article 3 could not be required to authorise killing. Nor is the state obliged to give someone who wants to kill themselves the equipment to do so (*Haas* v. *Switzerland* (2011)).

- **Article 8:** the right to respect for private and family life. The decision to commit suicide fell within Article 8. However, the law could interfere in the exercise of that right if necessary to protect vulnerable people who might otherwise be pressurised into committing suicide.

- **Article 14:** the right to protection from discrimination. Mrs Pretty argued that if she was fully able-bodied, she would be able to kill herself and the law would not prevent that, but because she needed the help of a third party, the law prohibited it. This, she claimed, amounted to discrimination on the grounds of disability. The ECtHR held that if there was any discrimination, this was justified by the need to protect vulnerable people from being manipulated into committing suicide.

While most of the discussion in connection with human rights has centred on the possibility of being permitted to engage in euthanasia or assisted suicide, there have also been attempts to use human rights analysis to require doctors to provide treatment when a person is near death.

KEY CASE

R (Burke) v. *GMC* [2005] 3 FCR 169

Concerning: whether a patient can obtain an order prohibiting the withdrawal of treatment

Facts

Mr Burke suffered from cerebellar ataxia. It was predicted that he would at some point in the future need to be given artificial nutrition and hydration to be kept alive. He was concerned that if he became incompetent, these might be withdrawn and he would die. He wanted an order prohibiting the withdrawal of any nutrition and hydration he required.

Legal principle

Where a patient is incompetent, the doctor must decide what treatment to provide based on what is in the patient's best interests. A patient had no right to demand a particular kind of treatment either when they are competent or incompetent. The court, therefore, refused to grant the order sought.

■ Severely disabled adults and children

Simply because the patient is a severely disabled adult or child does not change the legal position. It is still murder to do an act which causes the patient's death, with intention to cause death or grievous bodily harm. However, the disability can be relevant in a case involving an omission. As we saw earlier, in that case a doctor does not need to provide treatment that is not positively in the best interests of the patient. That is equally true where without the treatment the patient will die. In some cases, the courts have declared that if an individual is facing a quality of life which is 'intolerable', a doctor need not provide life-preserving or life-saving treatment (*Re J (A Minor) Re M* (1990)). Some recent cases have not liked the language of intolerability and have preferred simply asking whether the treatment would be in the patient's best interests (e.g. *Re Wyatt (A Child)* (*Medical Treatment: Continuation of Order*) (2005); *W* v. *M* (2011)). Where the doctors and the parents of a child patient disagree, the matter should be brought to court (*Glass* v. *UK* (2004)).

■ Ethical issues surrounding euthanasia

Much of the discussion of the ethical issues is confused by a failure to be clear about the terminology used.

KEY DEFINITION

Voluntary euthanasia. Conduct which has caused the patient's death at the patient's request.

Non-voluntary euthanasia. Conduct which causes the death of the patient without the patient's consent or objection (e.g. where the patient is in a coma and cannot consent).

Involuntary euthanasia. Conduct which kills the patient who is competent and has refused to consent to being killed.

Very few people support the idea of involuntary euthanasia. In fact, killing competent people without their consent is best described as murder. Much of the ethical dispute over euthanasia and connected issue concerns the notions of 'sanctity of life' and 'death with dignity'. Sanctity of life is the notion that life is a fundamental good. Life should be valued in itself. So even the life of a person suffering terrible disabilities should be treasured.

✎ EXAM TIP

Keown (2002) is adamant that the principle of sanctity of life should be kept distinct from the principle of vitalism. Vitalism says that it is never justifiable to kill another person and doctors should do everything possible to keep patients alive. Keown argues that the principle of sanctity of life means it is permissible to withhold treatment which is futile (e.g. it offers no hope of benefit) or to give treatment which will hasten the patient's death if it is not intended to kill the patient (but rather, for example, provide pain relief).

Opponents of euthanasia tend to emphasise the principle of autonomy. Put simply: people should be permitted to live their lives as they wish. Doing so protects their dignity. If I decide the time has come for me to die, then that is no one else's business but my own and other people should respect my decision. Indeed, the timing of death is a particularly personal matter and so is especially deserving of respect.

✓ Make your answer stand out

A good understanding of the academic debates surrounding the issues of euthanasia will impress the examiners. Keown (1995) has a good collection of essays from a variety of points of view on the issue. Dworkin (1993) gives a powerful case in favour of permitting euthanasia. Keown (2002) presents, with admirable clarity, the case against. Jackson and Keown (2011) provide an excellent presentation of the arguments on both sides of the debate.

When considering the debates surrounding euthanasia and related issues it is helpful to realise there are two kinds of arguments taking place. First, there are those at the level of principle. What, based on ethical principles, would be the best position for the law to take (e.g. Biggs; Dworkin)? Second, there are those based on practical considerations (e.g. George; Keown (2002)). Is it possible to produce a law which allows people who wish to die to do so, but protects vulnerable people from being taken advantage of? In this discussion, it is useful to refer to the experience of those countries which have permitted euthanasia or assisted suicide (e.g. The Netherlands; the state of Oregon in the USA).

■ Putting it all together

Answer guidelines

See the essay question at the start of the chapter.

Approaching the question

Notice the question asks you to summarise the law and consider reform. You are going to have a lot of material to cover. Be concise.

Important points to include

In this essay you need to summarise the law on this area. It is particularly important to structure your answer clearly. You will need to set out the law of murder as it applies in this context. Draw particular attention to the distinction between an act and an omission (discussing *Bland*). Remember that in relation to omissions it is permissible for a doctor to withdraw treatment if that treatment is not in the patient's best interests. You will also need to emphasise the significance of intention in this context (*Woollin*). A doctor may be permitted to administer treatment to a patient which will hasten the patient's death, if doing so is not the doctor's primary aim. You also need to emphasise that a competent patient has the right to refuse treatment, but not to demand it.

You are also asked whether it is logical to permit assisted suicide but not euthanasia. The argument in favour of such an approach is that with assisted suicide cases we can be confident that the individuals want to die (or can we?) because they have to administer the lethal substance to themselves. While with euthanasia there is a risk that although people might say they want to be killed, they may in fact not wish that (see *R (Purdy)* v. *DPP*). The arguments against would concentrate on those who are unable to kill themselves through disability. Is it fair that they are discriminated against by not permitting them to make the decision?

✓ Make your answer stand out

Show a good knowledge of the arguments that might be used on both sides of the debate. Jackson and Keown (2011) is written by two authors with very different views and so is well worth reading.

READ TO IMPRESS

Biggs, H. (2001) *Euthanasia, Death with Dignity and the Law*. Oxford: Hart.

Chau, P.-L. and Herring, J. (2007) 'The Meaning of Death', in Brooks-Gordan *et al. Death Rites and Rights*. Oxford: Hart.

Dworkin, R. (1993) *Life's Dominion*. London: Harper Collins.

George, K. (2007) 'A Woman's Choice? The gendered risks of voluntary euthanasia and physician-assisted suicide', 15 *Medical Law Review* 1.

Greasley, K. (2010) 'R (Purdy) v DPP and the Case for Wilful Blindness', 30 *Oxford Journal of Legal Studies* 301.

Herring, J. (2012) 'Escaping the Shackles of Law at the End of Life', 21 *Medical Law Review* 487.

Keown, J. (ed.) (1995) *Euthanasia Examined*. Cambridge: Cambridge University Press.

Keown, J. (1997) 'Restoring Moral and Intellectual Shape to the Law after *Bland*', 113 *Law Quarterly Review* 481.

Keown, J. (2002) *Euthanasia, Ethics and Public Policy*. Cambridge: Cambridge University Press.

Jackson, E. and Keown, J. (2011) *Debating Euthanasia*. Oxford: Hart.

McGee, A. (2011) 'Ending the Life of the Act/Omission Dispute: causation in withholding and withdrawing life-sustaining measures', 31 *Legal Studies* 467.

Michalowski, S. (2013) 'Relying on Common Law Defences to Legalise Assisted Dying: problems and possibilities', 21 *Medical Law Review* 337.

Mullock, A. (2011) 'Overlooking the Criminally Compassionate: what are the implications of prosecutorial policy on encouraging or assisting suicide?', 18 *Medical Law Review* 442.

Ost, S. (2010) 'The De-Medicalisation of Assisted Dying: is a less medicalised model the way forward?', 18 *Medical Law Review* 497.

www.pearsoned.co.uk/lawexpress

Go online to access more revision support including quizzes to test your knowledge, sample questions with answer guidelines, podcasts you can download, and more!

10

Mental health law

Revision checklist

Essential points you should know:

- [ ] When a person can be detained under the Mental Health Act 1983
- [ ] How the law protects the rights of those detained under the Mental Health Act 1983
- [ ] The reforms of the law in the Mental Health Act 2007

■ Topic map

■ Introduction

The Mental Health Act 2007 has reformed the law on mental illness.

Although there was widespread agreement that the law needed to be changed, it has taken over five years to enact new legislation. This reflects how controversial the topic is. Finding the correct balance between protecting the public from people who are regarded as potentially dangerous, and protecting the rights of mentally ill people, has proved difficult. The current law permits the detention of people who, although competent, suffer from a mental illness and pose a risk to themselves or others. There is much disagreement over when it is appropriate to do this. If someone has committed no offence, is it justifiable to detain a person simply because they are thought dangerous? But if a person is known to be dangerous and is left in the community, does this fail to protect the rights of any person subsequently attacked by them? Further, there is the issue of how a person detained under the Act should be treated and what rights they have.

ASSESSMENT ADVICE

Essay questions

These are likely to cover one or both of two issues. The first is when it is permissible to detain individuals under the Mental Health Act 1983 as amended by the 2007 Act. The second is how a person who is detained should be treated. You may also be required to discuss the recent reforms of the law. You will need to consider how the new Act has changed the law and whether it has struck the correct balance between protecting the mentally ill and protecting the public. As well as considering the details of the law, you will also need to consider the theoretical issues that arise: in particular, how the Human Rights Act impacts on mental health law and the debates over the justification for detaining competent mentally ill people.

Problem questions

These are likely to raise issues both relating to detention and treatment of mentally ill people. You will need to have a good knowledge of the different ways that a person can be detained under the Mental Health Act 1983, as amended by the 2007 Act, and be able to explain the different grounds that need to be shown to justify detention. A good answer will be able to discuss how a human rights challenge might be made in relation to some of the grounds. You will also need to be able to explain when a person can be discharged from detention under the 1983 Act.

■ Sample question

Could you answer this question? Below is a typical essay question that could arise on this topic. Guidelines on answering the question are included at the end of this chapter, whilst a sample problem question and guidance on tackling it can be found on the companion website.

ESSAY QUESTION

Does the current mental health law adequately protect the human rights of mentally ill people?

■ Who is covered by the Act?

The Mental Health Act 2007 has amended the Mental Health Act 1983 to mean that only those who suffer a **mental disorder** are covered by the legislation. If there are concerns about someone who does not suffer a mental disorder, then the Act cannot be used to assess or detain them (*DD* v. *Durham County Council* (2013)).

KEY DEFINITION: Mental disorder

A mental disorder is defined as 'any disorder or disability of the mind' (Mental Health Act 1983, section 1(2), as amended by the 2007 Act). The Act also refers to two things that are not mental disorders: learning disabilities and dependence on drugs or alcohol.

KEY STATUTE

Mental Health Act 1983, section 2(2)

An application for assessment may be made in respect of a patient on the grounds that –

(a) he is suffering from mental disorder of a nature or degree which warrants the detention of the patient in a hospital for assessment (or for assessment followed by medical treatment) for at least a limited period; and

(b) he ought to be so detained in the interests of his own health or safety or with a view to the protection of other persons.

KEY CASE

MH v. Secretary of State for Health **[2005] UKHL 60**

Concerning: whether section 2 of the MHA is compatible with human rights

Facts

M was a severely mentally disabled woman and was detained under section 2 of the Mental Health Act 1983. Under section 2 the burden lay on her to apply to the Mental Health Review Tribunal to review her detention. As M was incapable of doing this and there was a delay while her mother's application to be appointed a guardian was heard, on M's behalf it was claimed that the way section 2 placed the burden on her to bring her case before the Tribunal interfered with her rights under Article 5 of the ECHR.

Legal principle

The House of Lords held that section 2, MHA was compatible with the ECHR. Article 5 did not require that every detention be subject to judicial approval. The system under the MHA gave patients and relatives easy access to the Tribunal. Although a nearest relative had no right to apply to the Tribunal directly where that caused problems, there were means available to ensure that the Tribunal heard the case.

✎ EXAM TIP

Note that section 2 can be used where the detention is necessary in order to protect the patient, as well as where the risk is to other people. So a suicidal patient could be detained under this provision, although note that a person can only be detained for a maximum of 28 days.

■ Detention and treatment under section 3

This is the ground to be used if longer-term detention is required. An application can only be made by an approved social worker or the patient's nearest relative.

KEY STATUTE

Mental Health Act 1983, section 3(2)

An application for admission for treatment may be made in respect of a patient on the grounds that –

(a) he is suffering from a mental disorder of a nature or degree which makes it appropriate for him to receive medical treatment in a hospital; and

(b) it is necessary for the health or safety of the patient or for the protection of other persons that he should receive such treatment and it cannot be provided unless he is detained under this section; and

(c) appropriate medical treatment is available for him.

It should be noticed that section 3 is only available in relation to patients suffering a mental disorder of the kind mentioned. It is not sufficient just to show that the individual is a danger to themselves or others (*R (Sessay)* v. *South London and Maudsley NHS Trust* (2011)). Detention under section 3 is initially for six months and can be extended a further six months. Once detention is justified under section 3, yearly extensions are possible. A person can be detained under section 3 for the rest of their life. Continued detention requires a responsible medical officer to produce a report that indicates that the patient still suffers from a mental disorder and that treatment is necessary to prevent deterioration or alleviate the condition, or that the patient will not be able to care for themselves outside the hospital setting. The detention must be necessary for the health or safety of the patient or others. It is possible to challenge continued detention under section 3 by applying to a Mental Health Tribunal.

> **EXAM TIP**
>
> An issue which is well worth revising carefully is the requirement in section 3 that the condition be one where treatment must be able to improve or at least prevent the worsening of the condition if the person suffers from a psychopathic disorder or mental impairment. This means (controversially) that a person with a severe mental illness, who cannot be offered a treatment, cannot be detained. The argument in favour of this is that otherwise doctors would be keeping patients in hospitals they could offer no treatment to, but were, in effect, just incarcerating. The argument against is that it means that people who pose a danger to the public can be detained even though they have not harmed anyone.

Admission under section 4

Section 4 is for use in emergencies. Only a doctor can authorise admission under section 4 where the case is of an urgent necessity and that waiting for a second doctor's opinion (in order to admit under section 2) would cause undesirable delay. The maximum length that a person can be detained under section 4 is 72 hours. The idea is that when the section 4 order expires, either the patient is free to go home or section 2 or 3 would be used.

Treatment of patients

If a patient who has been detained is competent, they can consent to treatment and the normal rules apply. If, however, they are competent and refuse treatment then if they have been detained under the Mental Health Act, they can be given treatment for mental disorders but not for other physical conditions. The distinction between treatment for physical conditions and others is problematic.

Distinction drawn	Case
Forced feeding of someone suffering anorexia nervosa was permissible	*Re KB (Adult)* (1994)
An urgent Caesarean section on a schizophrenic woman, whose mental condition it was found would worsen if the baby died, was permissible	*Tameside and Glossop AST* v. *CH* (1996)
Treatment of a mental disorder which was not the disorder for which the person had been detained was permissible	*R (B)* v. *Ashworth Hospital* (2005)

📖 **REVISION NOTE**

Remember the issue is less complex where a person has lost their mental capacity. In that case, the person can be treated under the provisions of the Mental Capacity Act 2005 and given any treatment which is in their best interests (see Chapter 3).

■ Informal treatment

The Mental Health Act 2007 has inserted a new section 64 into the Mental Health Act 1983. This is to deal with cases where a patient is not being formally detained under the Act but is not resistant to receiving treatment for mental disorder. The treatment can be given if the patient is competent and consents, but also if the patient lacks capacity. The Act permits this if the five conditions in section 64D are met.

KEY STATUTE

Mental Health Act 1983, section 64D

(1) The first condition is that, before giving the treatment, the person takes reasonable steps to establish whether the patient lacks capacity to consent to the treatment.

(2) The second condition is that, when giving the treatment, he reasonably believes that the patient lacks capacity to consent to it.

(3) The third condition is that –

  (a) he has no reason to believe that the patient objects to being given the treatment; or

  (b) he does have reason to believe that the patient so objects, but it is not necessary to use force against the patient in order to give the treatment. ▶

(4) The fourth condition is that –

    (a) he is the person in charge of the treatment and an approved clinician; or

    (b) the treatment is given under the direction of that clinician.

(5) The fifth condition is that giving the treatment does not conflict with –

    (a) an advance decision which he is satisfied is valid and applicable; or

    (b) a decision made by a donee, deputy or the Court of Protection.

! Don't be tempted to . . .

It is important to realise that the law on necessity has been changed following the Human Rights Act. Prior to section 64D, the courts had relied on the common law principle of necessity. As the European Court of Human Rights (*HL* v. *UK* (2004)) noted, the law on the treatment of those treated on the basis of necessity was unclear. One of the aims of the new Mental Health Act is to clarify the circumstances in which treatment can be given for a mental condition where the person lacks capacity, but is not being detained.

■ Code of Practice

The Mental Health Act 2007 has amended the Mental Health Act 1983 to authorise the Secretary of State for Health to issue a Code of Practice. This Code of Practice is likely to become very influential in the way the law is applied. The Act sets down some principles which the Code should reflect.

KEY STATUTE

Mental Health Act 1983, section 118(2)

In preparing the statement of principles the Secretary of State shall, in particular, ensure that each of the following matters is addressed –

(a) respect for patients' past and present wishes and feelings;

(b) respect for diversity generally including, in particular, diversity of religion, culture and sexual orientation (within the meaning of section 35 of the Equality Act 2006);

(c) minimising restrictions on liberty;

(d) involvement of patients in planning, developing and delivering care and treatment appropriate to them;

(e) avoidance of unlawful discrimination;

(f) effectiveness of treatment;

(g) views of carers and other interested parties;

(h) patient wellbeing and safety; and

(i) public safety.

The Mental Health Act 2007

The progress of the Mental Health Act 2007 through Parliament was painfully slow. It was the subject of fierce debates and frequent changes. In the end, the extent of reform is much less than expected. The Act does little more than make some fairly minor changes to the 1983 Act. It may well be that the Code produced under the Act turns out to be far more influential than the Act itself.

The main changes in the Act are as follows. It provides a single definition of mental disorder which will apply through all the legislation. The issue which has raised the most controversy is whether a person can be detained under the Act even if no medical treatment is available for their mental disorder. The Act makes it clear that, under section 3, a person can only be detained if there is 'appropriate medical treatment' for them. In other words, if a person is recognised as dangerous, but no treatment is available, they cannot be detained under the Mental Health Act 1983, as amended. The significance of this is lessened by the amendment by the 2007 Act of the definition of treatment in section 145 of the 1983 Act. This now includes 'specialist mental health care'. It might be thought that anyone could benefit from 'care', and so if doctors believe a person poses a genuine risk to the public, they can be detained if 'care' can be offered. To be justified under section 145, the treatment does not have to render the patient less dangerous (*MD* v. *Nottinghamshire Health Care NHS Trust* (2010)). The Act contains a host of other minor amendments, including, most notably, the power to make community treatment orders.

✎ EXAM TIP

The issue which has so troubled Parliamentarians discussing the Mental Health Act 2007 is a difficult one. Is it permissible to detain a person suffering from a mental disorder who cannot be offered any treatment? In other words, is it appropriate that a person be detained simply to protect 'the public'? Doctors complain that if they detain a person they cannot treat, they are acting more like a prison than a hospital. On the other hand, if a person is known to be dangerous, should they be free to live among the public? In considering this issue, you should notice that doctors have found it extremely difficult to predict correctly who, if released, might injure someone else. See Bartlett (2003) and Fennell (2005) for a full discussion of these issues. There is also the further problem of overcrowding in prisons and ensuring that any prisoners who have mental health needs receive the treatment they need.

■ Putting it all together

Answer guidelines

See the essay question at the start of the chapter.

Approaching the question

There are a lot of issues which could be discussed here. It may be best to focus on some of the key rights and discuss those in depth, rather than discuss all of the issues which could be raised.

Important points to include

A good place to start in answering the question is to set out the main human rights issues that are raised in mental health law (e.g. *MH* v. *Secretary of State for Health*). These include the circumstances in which a person may be detained, the reasons for which a person may be detained, the treatment to be given to a person detained under the Act, and the legal position of those voluntarily receiving mental health treatment. Note that the ECHR requires there to be effective procedures to ensure that people can challenge their detention. In discussing these issues you will particularly want to address the rights under Article 3 to protection from inhuman or degrading treatment, and the right to respect for private or family life under Article 8. You will then need to look at the current law and discuss the extent to which the rights you have discussed are protected.

✓ Make your answer stand out

A good answer will emphasise why looking at these issues from a human rights perspective is important. Notice, in particular, the shift from focusing on the protection of the public, to focusing on the rights of those who are mentally ill.

READ TO IMPRESS

Bartlett, P. (2003) 'The Test of Compulsion in Mental Health Law: capacity, therapeutic benefit and dangerousness as possible criteria', 11 *Medical Law Review* 326.

Bartlett, P. and Sandland, R. (2003) *Mental Health Law: Policy and Practice*. Oxford: Oxford University Press.

Davidson, L. (2002) 'Human Rights versus Public Detention: English mental health law in crisis?', 25 *International Journal of Law and Psychiatry* 491.

Fennell, P. (2005) 'Convention Compliance, Public Safety and the Social Inclusion of Mentally Disordered People', 32 *Journal of Law and Society* 90.

McSherry, B. and Weller, P. (eds) (2010) *Rethinking Rights-Based Mental Health Laws*. Oxford: Hart.

Richardson, G. (2002) 'Autonomy, Guardianship and Mental Disorder: one problem, two solutions', 65 *Modern Law Review* 702.

Szmukler, G., Daw, R. and Dawson, J. (2010) 'A Model Law Fusing Incapacity and Mental Health Legislation', 11 *Journal of Mental Health Law* 12.

www.pearsoned.co.uk/lawexpress

Go online to access more revision support including quizzes to test your knowledge, sample questions with answer guidelines, podcasts you can download, and more!

Medical research

Revision checklist

Essential points you should know:

- [ ] What forms of medical research are outlawed
- [ ] When children and incapacitated adults can be involved in medical research
- [ ] How medical research is regulated

■ Topic map

■ Introduction

Volunteering to take part in medical research can be risky.

In 2006, six volunteers were left seriously ill after a trial for a new drug went wrong. Unfortunately, testing drugs on humans is essential if medical knowledge is to progress. The difficulties for the law is in where to draw the lines. What kinds of risks should volunteers be able to consent to? And what about children and incapacitated adults: can they be involved in medical research? The difficulty for the law has been in finding a form of regulation which adequately protects the interests of participants, but does not unduly hamper medical research.

ASSESSMENT ADVICE

Essay questions

These tend to focus on the legal regulation of healthcare research. You will need to have a good understanding of the formal legal restrictions as well as the work of the ethics committees. You might also be asked to discuss when and whether incompetent adults or children should be involved in research. You should be aware not only of the concerns that medical research is insufficiently regulated, but also of the concerns of researchers that their work is hampered by too many 'ethical' constraints.

Problem questions

This is not a particularly popular topic for a problem question. You might be asked about a case involving an incompetent person, or a volunteer for research which is particularly risky.

■ Sample question

Could you answer this question? Below is a typical essay question that could arise on this topic. Guidelines on answering the question are included at the end of this chapter, whilst a sample problem question and guidance on tackling it can be found on the companion website.

ESSAY QUESTION

Are there any good reasons why medical research should be subject to any special form of legal regulation, apart from the normal rules of the law of tort and crime?

Medical research

The only kinds of medical research which are regulated are those which involve one of the following:

- human subjects
- human sperm or eggs
- human embryos
- animals
- data relating to individuals.

So, research on just chemicals or bits of donated tissue are not regulated. When discussing this topic, it is important to draw a distinction between **therapeutic and non-therapeutic** research.

KEY DEFINITION: Therapeutic and non-therapeutic

A use of a drug will be therapeutic if it is given to a patient to provide treatment for a condition from which they will suffer. This is true even if a doctor is still conducting research on the effectiveness of the drug. Non-therapeutic use would be where the doctor expects no benefits to the patient to whom the treatment is given, but is giving them the treatment simply to record its side-effects or for other general research purposes.

EXAM TIP

The World Medical Association has produced the Declaration of Helsinki. This is not technically binding in English law, but is highly influential. Practitioners will regard themselves as bound by it and, where the law is unclear, courts are likely to refer to it. You should, therefore, know about it and be able to make reference to it in the exam. Its cardinal principle is that '[i]n medical research on human subjects, considerations related to the well-being of the human subjects should take precedence over the interests of science and society' (para. 5). The Declaration also emphasises the importance of having the consents of all subjects of research and the protection of the right of a subject to withdraw from any research project.

Regulation of research

General law

Of course, the criminal law must be complied with when conducting medical experiments. Giving a person a substance or touching them without their consent would be an offence, such as assault or battery. Similarly, the law of tort applies and so if as a result of a researcher's negligence a person suffers an injury then the researcher could be liable to pay compensation. There are also general statutes that can affect medical researchers, such as the Data Protection Act 1998 and Human Tissue Act 2004.

The consent of the participants is normally essential (although see below in relation to children and incompetent adults). It is important that research participants are given sufficient information about the research to be able to consent.

☐ REVISION NOTE

The law regarding consent has been discussed earlier (see Chapter 3). Particularly relevant in this context is that the participant must be informed of any significant risks if their consent to participate in the research is to be legally effective. One difficulty in practice is that research can be severely hampered if participants leave a project midway through. However, the principle of consent stipulates that the participants cannot be forced to receive treatment against their wishes. Although researchers might like to bind participants to be involved in the research until the end of the project, there is no legal way of doing this.

Research which is unlawful

Research which harms the participants

Research will not be permitted if it will endanger the lives of the subjects or cause them serious harm. The difficulty is in stating how much harm is permitted. No doubt the importance of the research will play a role. Research into finding a cure for cancer may be able to justify giving trial drugs to subjects which can cause nausea. It is unlikely that research into hair loss could justify a similar level of harm. It may also be relevant if the treatment being tested will have therapeutic benefits for the subjects.

KEY CASE

Simms v. *Simms* [2003] 1 All ER 669

Concerning: when experimental surgery was lawful

Facts

Two teenagers were suffering from variant Creutzfeldt-Jakob Disease. Their doctors proposed a novel treatment which had not been tested on humans. The expert evidence suggested that the effectiveness of the surgery was unknown. Without the treatment the individuals would die. Their parents sought a declaration that it was lawful for the proposed treatment to be given.

Legal principle

Butler-Sloss P authorised the surgery. As the two teenagers were incompetent to make the decision, the question was simply whether doing the surgery would be in their best interests. She held that it was. Although medical opinion was divided on whether or not the treatment should be given, the experts agreed it would not be irresponsible to give the treatment. The chance of success might be slight, but given they were facing death, it was a risk worth taking. She attached 'considerable weight' to the fact the parents supported using the treatment.

✓ Make your answer stand out

One issue that is well worth revising is whether there is a moral duty to participate in research (see Harris (2005) and Shapsay and Pimple (2007)). If you conclude that there is a moral duty to be involved in research, do you think this is stronger or weaker if the research relates to an illness from which you suffer? Regardless of whether there is a moral duty to be involved in research, could it affect your response as to whether the law should allow children or incapacitated adults to be involved?

Research involving children

This is a controversial subject. If the child is *Gillick* competent (see Chapter 3 for a discussion of this term), then they can probably consent to being a subject of research (although Lord Donaldson in *Re W* (1992) doubted this). If the child is not competent, the child's parents may be able to consent but parents, when making decisions for children, are meant to make their decisions for the benefit of the child, and if the treatment is non-therapeutic that may be questioned. Despite the uncertainty over the legality of research involving treatment, it clearly happens and needs to if children are to receive effective medication.

! Don't be tempted to . . .

This is a tricky issue and it is easy to get it wrong. If parents are meant to make decisions which are in the best interests of their child, is it permissible to consent to involve your child in a research project which might cause a small amount of discomfort but not directly benefit the child? You might say that it is in children's interests to grow up realising the benefits of helping other people. The difficulty is that if children are not involved in medical research, children as a group will be harmed because it cannot be assumed that medicine which is found to be safe for adults will also be safe for children.

Research involving incompetent adults

The law on research involving incompetent adults is set out in sections 30 to 34 of the Mental Capacity Act 2005. Notably, the Act only deals with intrusive research. So if the research does not involve touching or administering a substance (e.g. it just involved watching the subject), then the special regulations in the Act do not apply. If the treatment is intrusive, then the Act sets out a long list of requirements, which you should know for the exam. The most important of these are as follows.

Requirement for research on incompetent person (P)	Statute
The research must be related to a condition P suffers from	MCA, s. 31(1)
The research must either benefit P or be intended to assist people suffering from the same condition as P and the risk to P is negligible and the research not be unduly invasive	MCA, s. 31(5)
Nothing must be done to which P appears to object, unless that is necessary to protect P from harm	MCA, s. 33(2)
The research must be approved by an 'appropriate body' (e.g. the local ethics committee)	MCA, s. 30

The work of research ethics committees

All large-scale medical research must be approved by a research ethics committee. Although the committee will consider the legality of any research, it is, in theory, still open to a court to decide if the research was illegal. The committee will consider the likely validity of any research; whether participants will be caused any undue pain or discomfort; that the arrangements to ensure proper information is given; and consent obtained. The National Patient Safety Authority now oversees the work of ethics committees. It would be useful to visit their website (www.npsa.nhs.uk) to see the work it does and for more information, and to assess what factors committees should be taking into account.

■ Putting it all together

Answer guidelines

See the essay question at the start of the chapter.

Approaching the question

This question gives you a good opportunity to show your knowledge of the regulation of research and of the theoretical issues surrounding it. Your answer can be divided into two halves: the first looking at the current system of regulation and the second looking at how the law should regulate this area.

Important points to include

You should start this essay be explaining the ways in which the law regulates medical research, highlighting the point that, although the normal rules under criminal and tort law apply, there are additional regulations. In particular discuss the work of the research ethics committees.

You will also need to consider why there is a need for special regulation. Note that historically there have been terrible abuses of people in the name of medical research (see Plomer (2005, chapter 1)).

 Make your answer stand out

A good point to mention is that people are allowed to do a lot of risky things they like: for example, mountaineering or extreme ironing. If people can choose to do such risky activities, should they not be able to engage in the, arguably, more useful activity of research?

READ TO IMPRESS

Cave, E. (2010) 'Seen But Not Heard? Children in clinical trials', 18 *Medical Law Review* 1.

Dickert, N. (2009) 'Re-Examining Respect for Human Research Participants', 19 *Kennedy Institute of Ethics Journal* 311.

Ferguson, P. (2008) 'Clinical Trials and Healthy Volunteers', 16 *Medical Law Review* 23.

Foster, C. (2001) *The Ethics of Medical Research on Humans*. Cambridge: Cambridge University Press.

Fox, M. (1998) 'Research Bodies: feminist perspectives on clinical research', in S. Sheldon and M. Thomson (eds), *Feminist Perspectives in Health Care Law*. London: Cavendish.

Harris, J. (2005) 'Scientific Research is a Moral Duty', 31 *Journal of Medical Ethics* 291.

Laurie, G. and Postan, E. (2013) 'Rhetoric or Reality: what is the legal status of the consent form in health-related research?', 21 *Medical Law Review* 371.

McHale, J. (2006) 'Law Reform, Clinical Research and Adults without Mental Capacity', in S. McLean (ed.), *First Do No Harm*. Aldershot: Ashgate.

Plomer, A. (2005) *The Law and Ethics of Medical Research*. London: Cavendish.

Shapsay, S. and Pimple, K. (2007) 'Participation in Biomedical Research is an Imperfect Moral Duty: a response to John Harris', 33 *Journal of Medical Ethics* 414.

www.pearsoned.co.uk/lawexpress

Go online to access more revision support including quizzes to test your knowledge, sample questions with answer guidelines, podcasts you can download and more!

And finally, before the exam . . .

By this stage you should be well advanced with your revision. If you have worked through this book and used it to provide a structure for your revision notes, you will be on course to do well in the exams.

A few final words of advice. Remember to use the case law as much as possible. This will make sure you convince the examiner that you know the law as well as being able to discuss the theory. It will also mean that when you are talking about more theoretical points they will be grounded in real practical examples and not become too 'airy fairy'.

Remember also the limitations of the law. Law works through using rules. These are used to ensure consistent decisions are made and to provide guidance for professionals and others. This means that sometimes the law cannot work in as nuanced a way as some ethicists would like. Sometimes the law will sacrifice producing the ideal result in every case, in order to produce a clear rule which will work well in the vast majority of cases.

A final point is that medical law is meant to be interesting and excite strong reactions. In essay questions you should make it clear what you think the law should be and what the ethically correct approach is. However, make sure you are able to describe a variety of different views. If they are views you disagree with, explain what you see as their main weaknesses.

Test yourself

☐ Look at the **revision checklists** at the start of each chapter. Are you happy that you can now tick them all? If not, go back to the particular chapter and work through the material again. If you are still struggling, **seek help** from your tutor.

☐ Attempt the **sample questions** in each chapter and check your answers against the guidelines provided.

☐ Go online to **www.pearsoned.co.uk/lawexpress** for more hands-on revision help and try out these resources:

▶

- [ ] Try the **test your knowledge** quizzes and see if you can score full marks for each chapter.

- [ ] Attempt to answer the **sample questions** for each chapter within the time limit and check your answers against the guidelines provided.

- [ ] Listen to the **podcast** and then attempt the question it discusses.

- [ ] **'You be the marker'** and see if you can spot the strengths and weaknesses of the sample answers.

- [ ] Use the **flashcards** to test your recall of the legal principles of the key cases and statutes you've revised and the definitions of important terms.

- [ ] Watch out for medical issues in the newspapers.

- [ ] Discuss controversial medical issues with your friends, especially those who may disagree with you.

■ Linking it all up

Check where there are overlaps between subject areas. (You may want to review the 'revision note' boxes throughout this book.) Make a careful note of these as knowing how one topic may lead into another can increase your marks significantly. Here are some examples.

- ✔ The importance of autonomy
- ✔ Whether the law should uphold moral values
- ✔ Whether lawyers or doctors determine what treatment a patient should receive
- ✔ The role rationing plays

Notice that these themes appear in many topics. In particular the relationship between autonomy and upholding moral principles is a key one: should abortion be regarded as simply the choice of the woman; or should society uphold the moral value attached to a fetus?; is euthanasia a private matter for each individual or should the law protect the sanctity of life?; should an informed adult be allowed to participate in any research project; or should we restrict medical research which endangers participants? Another key theme is the extent to which judges should leave medical decisions to doctors or whether the law should intervene. We see that particularly in relation to the law on clinical negligence, where judges show deference to the views of medical experts. By contrast, the courts have shown an increasing willingness to intervene in cases involving decisions over rationing.

■ Knowing your cases

Make sure you know how to use relevant case law in your answers. Use the table below to focus your revision of the key cases in each topic. To review the details of these cases, refer back to the particular chapter.

Key case	How to use	Related topics
Chapter 1 – Basic principles of medical law and ethics		
St George's NHS Trust v. *S*	To show the importance of autonomy	Pregnancy; abortion
Simms v. *Simms*	To illustrate the 'do no harm' principle	Research
Chapter 2 – Rationing		
R v. *Cambridge HA ex p. B*	To show how courts are reluctant to intervene in rationing decisions	Children
R (Condliff) v. *North Staffordshire PCT*	To discuss how the courts balance the interests of patients and the community	Obesity
R v. *North West Lancashire HA ex p. A*	To give an example of a court finding a rationing policy unlawful	Gender
R (Rogers) v. *Swindon NHS PCT*	To illustrate when exceptional circumstances may be considered	Cancer
R (Watts) v. *Secretary of State for Health*	To demonstrate relevance of European law	EU law
Chapter 3 – Consent to treatment		
Re C (Adult: Refusal of Treatment)	To show the right to refuse treatment	Mental health
A Local Authority v. *Mrs and Mr A*	To provide an example of a person lacking capacity	Contraception
Sidaway v. *Bethlem Royal Hospital Governors*	To discuss what information a doctor should disclose	Autonomy
Chester v. *Afshar*	To examine when damages can be paid after failure to disclose	Negligence

▶

Key case	How to use	Related topics
Re Y (Mental Incapacity: Bone Marrow Transplant)	To consider 'best interests' principle	Organ donation
Chapter 4 – Confidentiality		
Campbell v. *MGN*	To demonstrate when a duty of confidence is owed	Human rights
R v. *Department of Health ex p. Source Informatics*	To consider if confidence is owed where the information is anonymous	Privacy
W v. *Edgell*	To illustrate when breach of confidence can be justified	Mental health
Chapter 5 – Medical negligence		
Bolam v. *Friern Hospital Management Committee*	To discuss duty of care in medical negligence cases	Patients' rights
Hotson v. *E. Berkshire AHA*	To examine when a loss of a chance claim may succeed	Damages
Gregg v. *Scott*	To consider loss of a chance cases	Damages
Chester v. *Afshar*	To illustrate when damages may be ordered after a failure to disclose risk	Consent
Chapter 6 – Contraception, abortion and pregnancy		
R (Smeaton) v. *Secretary of State for Health*	To define contraception	Embryos
A, B and C v. *Ireland*	To discuss whether there is a right to abortion	Human rights
R (Axon) v. *Secretary of State for Health*	To consider when minors can be given abortions	Parental rights
St George's Healthcare Trust v. *S*	To show the autonomy rights of pregnant women	Consent

Key case	How to use	Related topics
Chapter 7 – Reproduction		
Evans v. *Amicus*	To illustrate how the courts resolve disputes over frozen embryos	Human rights
R (Quintavalle) v. *HFEA*	To examine the legality of embryo selection	Embryos
Chapter 8 – Organ donation and ownership of body parts		
Yearworth v. *North Bristol NHS Trust*	To discuss whether someone owns their body parts	Reproduction
Chapter 9 – Death and dying		
R (Nicklinson) v. *Ministry of Justice*	To confirm that necessity is not a defence to murder in euthanasia cases	Necessity
Airedale NHS Trust v. *Bland*	To define death	Persistent vegetative state
Re B (Adult: Refusal of Medical Treatment)	To give an example of the right to refuse treatment	Omissions
R (Pretty) v. *DPP*	To illustrate the role of human rights in end-of-life decisions	Human rights
R (Purdy) v. *DPP*	To discuss the role of human rights in end-of-life decisions	Criminal law
R (Burke) v. *GMC*	To examine whether there is a right to be kept alive	Rationing
Chapter 10 – Mental health		
MH v. *Secretary of State for Health*	To illustrate significance of human rights in mental health law	Human rights
Chapter 11 – Medical research		
Simms v. *Simms*	To examine when experimental treatment can be used	'Do no harm' principle

Glossary of terms

The glossary is divided into two parts: key definitions and other useful terms. The key definitions can be found within the chapter in which they occur, as well as in the glossary below. These definitions are the essential terms that you must know and understand in order to prepare for an exam. The additional list of terms provides further definitions of useful terms and phrases which will also help you answer examination and coursework questions effectively. These terms are highlighted in the text as they occur but the definition can only be found here.

◼ Key definitions

Advance decision	An advance decision is a decision by a patient made about the treatment they wished to receive, or not to receive, if they lost capacity. It must have been made when the patient was over 18 and had capacity. The advance decision only becomes effective when the patient loses capacity.
Consequentialism	This approach decides whether an act is ethically right or wrong by looking at its consequences. Quite simply, if it produces more good than bad, the act is ethically right.
Contraception	A procedure or device which prevents fertilisation of the egg or the implantation of the fertilised egg.
Deontology	This approach says that it is right or wrong to infringe certain principles, regardless of the consequences. For example, some people believe it is never right to intentionally kill another person, however much good may be produced as a result.
Duty of care	In the law of tort, a person owes a duty of care to all those whom that person may foreseeably harm. Occasionally the courts hold that there are good public policy reasons for not finding a duty of care.
Ethic of care	This is an ethical approach which emphasises that we all live in relationship with other people and are dependent upon other people. It, therefore, is not possible to look at a patient and ask what rights they have as a lone individual or what is best for them. Rather we need to ask what is best for this group of people who are in relationship together. It values interdependency and mutuality over individual freedom.

Genetic information	This is medical information about your genes, including your DNA. This can reveal whether you have a genetically related illness or whether you are a carrier of one.
Gillick competent child	A child who has sufficient maturity and understanding to make a competent decision about the issue. The child will need to understand not only the medical issues involved, but also the moral and family questions.
Involuntary euthanasia	Conduct which kills the patient who is competent and has refused to consent to being killed.
Mental disorder	'Any disorder or disability of the mind' (MHA 1983, section 1(2), as amended by the 2007 Act). The MHA refers to two things that are not mental disorders: learning disabilities and dependence on drugs or alcohol.
Non-voluntary euthanasia	Conduct which causes the death of the patient without the patient's consent or objection (e.g. where the patient is in a coma and cannot consent).
Principle of beneficence	Medical professionals must provide the best medical treatment for their patients.
Principle of justice	Patients should be treated equally and fairly. One patient should not be improperly given preferential treatment over others.
Principle of non-malfeasance	Medical professionals should not cause harm to their patients.
Quality adjusted life year	This is an assessment of the benefit of a treatment. It takes into account how many years' extra life a treatment may provide and the increase in quality of life that a treatment may provide.
Rationing	Where there is only a limited healthcare resource and a decision must be made to offer the resources to some patients and not others.
Regenerative bodily material	This is body material which (if taken from a body) will be naturally replaced by the body. Blood or bone marrow would be good examples. Non-regenerative material will not be replaced by the body. Examples would be a heart or kidney.
Relevant material	The HTA 2004 only covers the use and storage of 'relevant material'. This is tissue, cells and organs of human beings. It does not include sperm, eggs or embryos. Cell lines or other human material created in a laboratory are not covered.
Reproductive autonomy	Supporters of reproductive autonomy argue that the decisions people make about whether or not to have children are intimate and profoundly important. The state should assist couples in their choice. Where a person or a couple wishes to have a child,

the state should assist them as far as is possible (given other restraints on resources). It is not the state's job to decide whether a person will make a good or bad parent or to restrict the way a person wishes to create a child. Sometimes the concept is distinguished from 'reproductive liberty' where, while the state should not prevent someone having a child, it is not under a positive obligation to assist them.

Res ipsa loquitur	Literally translated this means 'the act speaks for itself'. It is a doctrine used in the law of negligence where there is no reasonable explanation for an injury apart from the fact the defendant must have caused the injury negligently. In such a case the court will assume the defendant's negligence caused the injury even though that has not positively been proved.
Right	The concept of a right in law is much disputed and it is not possible to give a definition which would be accepted by everyone. When a person has a right to X, other people are bound by a duty to protect or promote the interests the person has in X. There need to be good reasons why the person should be prevented from X.
Surrogacy	One woman (the surrogate mother) agrees to carry a child for another woman or a couple (the commissioning couple). Their intention is that shortly after birth the child will be handed over to the commissioning couple and they will raise the child.
Therapeutic and non-therapeutic	A use of a drug will be therapeutic if it is given to a patient to provide treatment for a condition from which they will suffer. This is true even if a doctor is still conducting research on the effectiveness of the drug. Non-therapeutic use would be where the doctor expects no benefits to the patient to whom the treatment is given, but is giving them the treatment simply to record its side-effects or for other general research purposes.
Voluntary euthanasia	Conduct which has caused the patient's death at the patient's request.

▮ Other useful terms

Actus reus	The part of the definition of a crime that refers to the conduct of the defendant.
Mens rea	The part of the definition of a crime that refers to the mental state of the defendant.

Index

Note: page numbers in **bold** refer to
glossary entries.

abortion 67
  courts: orders to stop 74–5
  criminal offences 69–70
  ethics of 10, 75–6
  lawful 70–3
  legal status of fetus 75–6
  'morning after pill' 68–9
  pregnant woman lacking capacity 74
  right to 70, 73–4
  statutory grounds for 71–3
  under-16-year-olds and 74–5
  virtue ethics 10
access to medical information 50
actus reus 108, **148**
adoption 81, 87
advance decisions 27, 35, 128, **146**
  ethics of 35
  life-shortening treatment 113
  previous expression of views 39
  to refuse life-saving treatment 35, 113
age discrimination 22
alcohol dependence 124
anonymity of sperm donors 89
anonymous information 46–7
anorexia nervosa 127
assault 11
autonomy 5–6, 7, 8, 27, 29, 34
  euthanasia 117
  reproductive 81, 82–3, **147–8**

bailment 103
battery 32, 136
beneficence 7

best interests test 31, 35, 36–7, 116, 127
  abortion 74
  bodily material 99, 101
  medical research and children 137
  omission causing death 111, 112, 116
  previous expression of views 39
blood transfusion 38
body parts, ownership of 96–7, 102–3, 104
Bolam test 33, 54–5, 56–8
brain-stem death 109

Caesarean section 5, 34, 76, 127
capacity 30–1, 34
  abortion: pregnant woman lacking 74
  bodily material and lack of 99, 101
  deprivation of liberty and lacking 37
  medical research and lack of 136–8
  potential and actual 30
  treatment of adults lacking 34–7, 39, 76, 111,
      112, 116, 127–8, 138
carers 10
  see also relatives
casuistry 9
children
  assisted reproduction: welfare of 86
  bodily material, use or storage of 99, 101
  consent to treatment 37–8, 74–5, 137
  donating organs 101
  family life 9
  Gillick competent child 37, 38, 137, **147**
  medical research 137
  newborn babies 76
  one parent consents 38
  right to know genetic origins 89
  severely disabled 116
  under-16-year-olds and abortion 74–5

cholera 34
civil partners 90–2
clinical trials 99
codes of practice
  confidentiality 44
  mental health law 128–9
community treatment orders 129
compensation *see* damages
confidentiality 43–6
  consequentialism and deontology 4
  disclosure permitted 46–9
  genetic information 49, **147**
  guidelines from professional bodies 46
  right not to know 49
  right to access information 50
consent
  assisted reproduction 88–90
  bodily material 98–9, 100–2
  frozen embryos 85–6
  to information disclosure 46
consent to treatment 27–32
  advance decisions *see separate entry*
  autonomy 5–6, 27, 29, 34
  children 37–8, 74–5, 137
  clear decision 32
  competence 30–1
  incompetent adults 30–1, 34–7, 39, 76, 111,
    112, 116, 127–8, 138
  information 27, 30, 31–3
  medical research 135, 136–8
  mental health law 126–8
  negligence 32–3
  refuse treatment, right to *see separate*
    entry
  religious perspectives 11
  substituted judgement 36
  undue influence 32
  unwise decisions 29
consequentialism 4, **146**
contraception 31, 68–9, **146**
contract
  breach of 44
  surrogacy 87, 88, **148**
criminal law
  abortion 69–73
  bodily material 98, 99, 100–1, 102
  confidentiality 44

consent to treatment 32
  ending of life 110–15, 116
  medical research 135–6
  organ donation 100–1
  traffic offences 48

damages/compensation 62, 103
  negligence 61, 113, 136
data protection 136
death and dying 108–9
  body of deceased 99, 101–2
  criminal law 110–15, 116
  definition of death 109
  ethical issues and euthanasia 117–18
  human rights 111, 112, 115–16
  mercy killing 110, 113
  omissions causing death 111–13,
    116
  pain-relieving drugs 110, 111, 117
  severe disability 116, 117
Declaration of Helsinki 135
defensive medicine 54
deontology 4, **146**
dignity 9, 108, 117
diminished responsibility 113
disability 18
  discrimination 73
  learning disabilities 124
  severe 116, 117
discrimination 9
  death 115–16
  disability 73
  rationing 22, 23
disease, notifiable 34
drug dependence 124

embryos
  frozen 85–6
  HTA 2004 97
  medical research 135
  selection 86–7
emergencies 37, 126
employers 49
equality 18
  see also discrimination
equitable breach of confidence 44–5
ethic of care 10, **146**

ethical principles 3, 5, 11–12
  autonomy 5–6, 7, 8, 27, 29, 34, 117
  beneficence 7
  capacity 30
  casuistry 9
  consequentialism 4, **146**
  deontology 4, **146**
  dignity 9, 108, 117
  euthanasia 117–18
  feminist medical ethics 10
  justice 8
  non-malfeasance 6–7
  religious perspectives 11
  rights 8–9, **148**
  virtue ethics 10
ethics of abortion 10, 75–6
ethics of advance decisions 35
ethics committees 138
European Union law 22
euthanasia *see* death and dying
exam tips
  abortion 70, 71, 73
  advance decisions 35, **146**
  beneficence 7
  confidentiality 44, 46, 48
  consent to treatment 30, 32, 35
  death and dying 112, 113, 117, 118
  medical research 135
  mental health law 125, 126, 129
  negligence 57, 62
  organ donation and ownership of body parts 99
  rationing 18, 19, 21, **147**
  reproduction 86, 88, 89
experimental surgery 7, 136–7

family life *see* private and family life (Art 8)
feminist medical ethics 10, 75
forced feeding 127
freedom of expression 45, 46

gender reassignment surgery 20, 21
genetic information 49, **147**
Gillick **competent child** 37, 38, 137, **147**
good faith 47

Hippocratic oath 43
HIV positive healthcare professional 49

HIV positive patient
  confidentiality 4, 48
Human Fertilisation and Embryology Authority
    (HFEA) 84, 87
human rights 8, 9
  abortion 70, 73–4, 75, 76
  confidentiality 44, 45, 46
  death and dying 111, 112, 115–16
  frozen embryos 85
  mental health law 125, 128, 130
  sperm donors 89
Human Tissue Authority 99, 101

information
  anonymous 46–7
  confidentiality *see separate entry*
  consent to treatment 27, 30, 31–3
  genetic 49, **147**
  medical research 136
  negligence: failure to warn of a risk 32–3,
      60–1
  proposed organ donors 101
  right not to know 49
  right to access 50
  sperm donors 89
inhuman or degrading treatment 9, 112, 115,
    130
insurers 49

Jehovah's Witnesses 38
judicial review 19, 21
justice 8

learning disabilities 124
liberty
  adult lacking capacity being deprived
      of 37
  right to (Art 5) 125
licensing of medicines 62
life, right to 9, 75, 76
  death 114, 115
  withdrawal of treatment 112
life, sanctity of 117

manslaughter 113
margin of appreciation 85

medical research 99, 134–5
  children 137
  Declaration of Helsinki 135
  experimental surgery 7, 136–7
  moral duty 137
  regulation of 135–8, 139
  research ethics committees 138
  therapeutic and non-therapeutic 135, **148**
  unlawful 136–7
medicines, licensing of 62
mens rea 108, **148**
mental health law 123–4
  admission in emergencies (s 4) 126
  assessment and detention (s 2) 124–5
  Code of Practice 128–9
  community treatment orders 129
  dangerous but no available treatment 126,
    129
  detention and treatment (s 3) 125–6
  human rights 125, 128, 130
  informal treatment 127–8
  mental disorder 124, 126–7, 129, **147**
  Mental Health Act 2007 129
  time limits 125, 126
  treatment of patients 126–7, 129
  Tribunal 126
mercy killing 110, 113
miscarriage 68–9
moral duty and medical research 137
'morning after pill' 68–9
murder 110–11, 113, 116, 117

National Patient Safety Authority 138
necessity
  abortion 70
  euthanasia 110–11
  mental health 128
  treatment of children 37
negligence 54–6, 113
  Bolam test 33, 54–5, 56–8
  breach of duty of care 56–8
  causation 58–61
  confidentiality 44
  damages 61, 113, 136
  duty of care 56, **146**
  failure to warn of a risk 32–3, 60–1
  harm to secondary victims 61

  loss of a chance 54, 55, 58–60
  medical research 136
  no fault scheme 54, 62
  psychological distress 61
  redress schemes 54, 61–2
  res ipsa loquitur 58, **148**
Netherlands 118
NHS Constitution 22
NICE (National Institute for Health
    and Clinical Excellence)
    17–18, 21
no fault scheme 54, 62
non-malfeasance 6–7
notifiable disease 34

organ donation 96–7
  children donating 101
  consent 98–9, 100–2
  definition of death 109
  incompetent adult 101
  living adult donors 100–1
  'opt out' system 102
  rationing 15
  regenerative bodily material 100, **147**
  relevant material 97, **147**
  selling organs 9, 102
  transplants from the dead 101–2
overseas hospitals 22

parentage
  assisted reproduction 88–92
  parental orders 87–8
persistent vegetative state 112
police investigations
  confidentiality 48–9
power of attorney 35
pregnancy 67–8
  abortion *see separate entry*
  Caesarean section 5, 34, 76, 127
  legal status of fetus 75–6
  regulation of 76
press freedom 49
prisons 129
privacy 44, 47
private and family life (Art 8) 9, 46, 85
  death 115
  mental health law 130

professional bodies 44, 46, 62
proportionality 37
public interest
  disclosure of information 48
  euthanasia 113
  negligence 62

quality adjusted life years (QALYs) 17–18, **147**

rationing 15–17, **147**
  autonomy 5
  beneficence 7
  'exceptional' cases 20, 21
  judicial challenges 19–22
  justice 8
  NICE 17–18, 21
  QALYs 17–18, **147**
redress schemes 54, 61–2
refuse treatment, right to
  autonomy 5, 6, 29, 34
  Caesarean section 5, 34, 76
  children 38
  exceptions 34
  mental disorders 126–7
  private life 9
  ventilator switched off 112–13
regulation by professional or NHS bodies 62
relatives
  body of deceased 99, 101–2, 104
  ethic of care 10
  euthanasia 113
  mental health law 125
  negligence: harm to secondary victims 61
religion 11, 36, 38, 76
reproduction 81–2
  civil partner of a mother 90–2
  embryo selection 86–7
  frozen embryos 85–6
  HFEA licence to make lawful 84, 87
  no licence required 85
  parentage 88–92
  reproductive autonomy 81, 82–3, **147–8**
  restrictions to treatment 86–8

surrogacy 87–8, **148**
  techniques of assisted 83–4
  unlawful activities 84
res ipsa loquitur 58, **148**
research *see* medical research
residence orders 87
rights 8–9, **148**
  to access information 50
  not to know 49

social workers 125
statutory obligation, breach of 44
substituted judgement 36
suicide 34, 111, 114
  assisted 114–16, 118
  detention of suicidal patient 125
  private and family life (Art 8) 115
surrogacy 87–8, **148**

taxation 17
theft 98
time limits
  mental health law 125, 126
tort law
  battery 32
  bodily material 98
  medical research 136
  negligence *see separate entry*
traffic offences 48
transsexualism 20, 21

undue influence 32
United States 118

virtue ethics 10
vitalism 117
vulnerable people 34, 115–16, 118

withdrawal from research project 135, 136
withdrawal of treatment
  ethical issues 117
  omission causing death 111, 112, 116
  order prohibiting 116
World Medical Association 135